EL'S RAE: A MEMOIR

Ellen Wallace Douglas

Order this book online at www.trafford.com
or email orders@trafford.com

Most Trafford titles are also available at major online book retailers.

Also by author: The Laughing Christ, Trafford, 2002

Photo of author in clergy collar with permission of The Country Studio, Albany, NY

Contact author by email: reverendellen@yahoo.com

Print information available on the last page.

ISBN: 978-1-4120-6542-9 (sc)

Trafford rev. 11/25/2019

Trafford
PUBLISHING® www.trafford.com
North America & international
toll-free: 1 888 232 4444 (USA & Canada)
fax: 812 355 4082

DEDICATION

This book is dedicated to my four children: Evie, Roy, Marty and Wendy; my grandchildren: Owen, Stephanie, Nick, Shane, Jillian, Jeffrey, Bryan, Katie and Michael; my great-grandchildren: Jocee and Kylee.

"Remember always that you have not only the right to be an individual, you have the obligation to be one. You cannot make any useful contributions to life unless you do that."

- Eleanor Roosevelt

CONTENTS

Foreword

Everyone's life is a story. A story characterized by who we are - and that in itself is no small thing. We are each a product of our inherited genetics, our particular parents, our cultural ethos, our education, our opportunities. And that product, that amalgam of who we **are** is further colorated by events and individuals - be they negative or positive. To modify John Donne's sage observation, No person is an island. We are a part of all we have met, and all we have met becomes a part of us.

One need not be a statesman, a celebrity, an individual of particular talent or accomplishment (or lack thereof!), a victim or conqueror to feel a need to compose one's memoir. Today, indeed, for the past decade, colleges, Continuing Education programs, writing workshops all tout offerings in memoir writing. Book stores offer memoirs inspired by occupations, war, eureka moments, or by whatever affects the human condition.

Why does one write a memoir? Sometimes it is to purge the self of demons. One may also write to leave a record, a record that is of interest to the writer but which may also greatly benefit the intended audience. Some of us write to create. It is part of the process of discovering and understanding ourselves. And sometimes we write not just to define the past but to capture the moment.

It takes a great deal of courage to write about the influences, motivations, and events in one's life; the sorrows and joys, the mistakes, the shames, the screw-ups and regrets. To reveal them not only to one's children and grandchildren, to friends and acquaintances, but also to the world- for to publish is to announce- one must bare one's soul. Not all of us can, or wish, to draw upon the courage needed for that creative process.

But Ellen Wallace Douglas is one of those exceptions. Her purpose in writing of her life was to leave a legacy of understanding to those she loves. An understanding of the times and circumstances and the world into which she was born and matured. And, very importantly to her, she shares an awareness of the spiritual influences and beliefs which have sustained "God's child" in her older, more enlightened years. She has succeeded in her endeavor and I have enjoyed, and learned from, the adventure and the journey with her.

Vincenza Pentick, Editor
May 2005

PREFACE

I wrote this book primarily to bring to the attention of the readers the story of my spiritual path. We all are on a spiritual path, uniquely designed, back home to God. Mine took me from my home area when I was in my forties and presented me with the opportunity to hear a master teacher as he brought forth the truth of our being, the reason for our being and the route home to God. I was joined in that great adventure with several other people who were also ready to hear the wisdom of the ages presented. Thus it was that halfway through my life my spiritual path opened onto a brilliant vista of learning, a broad scope of truth, and a "straightening of the crooked places," as Jesus put it, and the correcting of undeliberate errors of the early religious teachings. Words fail me when I attempt to express the joy, the love, the peace and the tenderness which accompanied all the lessons taught by Archangel Gabriel and Master Jesus. There were those unready for the lessons, but the teacher made it clear that that was not important. Some day they would be ready, for it is clearly stated in *A Course in Miracles*, "This is a required course." But the time when one accepts its teachings is chosen by the reader, in this lifetime or another.

My other reason for writing my life story is that two of my children suggested that I do so, in order for my grandchildren to know me better. I have attempted to draw a picture of myself which is true. I did my best. It is said that everyone has a story to write. It is my hope that mine is worth reading about. It was worth living, the early part which brought the joys of parenthood (in spite of the tragic episode of alcoholism), and the last half of it, full of learning eternal truths and in turn writing about them, lecturing about them and to the best of my ability, living them. From this richer and more self-critical perspective I know now that life is a continuum; that there is no death, and that I chose my path. Only when I pass over into the next plane of existence will I know how well I succeeded with my plan.

Since this is the story of my life, there was little research to be done. I did spend many hours at the Monroe County Clerk's office to find out how much property my father owned before the Great Depression. I went to the Historical Societies of Waterloo and Seneca Falls, my mother's hometown, to learn about the Red Jacket monument which her father worked on as a stone mason. My sister Mertice's audiocassette tape which I recorded in 2001, three years before she passed into spirit, supplied me with information I didn't know before, including a story about our brother Blake. My sister Joy wrote a diary and a copy of a portion of it, written in 1980, was given to me by her daughter Jean. It revealed the great effort which Joy invested in taking her employer to court in a sex-discrimination suit over wage differential between the male and female employees. She won, but she paid a high price as she continued in employment for her adversary.

I would like to thank my children Wendy and Marty for suggesting that I write this story. Knowing I had their support helped me to pursue long-past, nearly-forgotten experiences and write them down. Because of the traumatic episodes, this book would not even have been considered by me had I not spent hours and hours in counseling, dealing with painful experiences of my childhood, purging my feelings so that I could recall my life without pain. Through the counseling I was enabled to express the anger and hurt hidden in my memory. That is the goal of counseling, and I am very grateful to all the counselors who helped me throughout my life.

The people who were there for me through the years know who they are. It would be impossible for me to name them all. Some of my most profound lessons were learned from people I can not name, at a time I can not recall. Perhaps this book will help others even though to me they may remain unnamed and unknown.

xi

Special acknowledgement is given to my dear friend and editor, Mrs. Vincenza Pentick for her unending patience, devoted attention and sincere interest in my writing. Her generous offer of extensive time and literary expertise are appreciated beyond measure.

Particular acknowledgement is given to my niece Jean Zimber for critiquing the manuscript and suggesting in several instances that she wanted me to write "more"; to Jean Schaefer Cameron, lifelong friend, who read the draft and made valuable recommendations.

General and grateful acknowledgement is given to Donna Taylor, Danny Bailey, Carol Gottfried and Shirley Miller for their interest in my life's story and their willingness to read an early draft of the book; to Mariah Perkins, Sheila Galbraith and Marylou Krywe for their efficient and enthusiastic assistance in proofreading the manuscript with me.

Sincere acknowledgement is given to my beloved friend Donald Anthony who transmitted the manuscript to the publisher. He did so efficiently and willingly, as well as with enthusiastic support of me and my writing efforts.

The title of this book is derived from the ancient Hebrew word for God, "El," and my middle given name which is Rae. I am a child of God, as is all of humanity. Hence the title "El's Rae."

E.W.D.

May 2005

Chapter 1: Childhood

1928 - 1949; Age Birth to 20

It was Christmas night, 1928, and my mother was on her way to Rochester General Hospital to give birth to her ninth child, me. The hospital building is no longer there.
It was razed and a new hospital was built on the north side of the city and it, too, was called Rochester General. It was only a short distance from our home on Hobart St. Mother was in hard labor for many hours, and I was not delivered into this world until the evening of December 26. A few hours after my birth Dad said to her, "No more, Momma." He was sweating from his deep concern and distress over her extended labor. Fathers were not allowed in the delivery room in those days, so he had paced, worried, as all fathers did. She had given him nine healthy children. He loved children. But this would be the last, he knew. He couldn't see her go through this again, ever. Al, their previous child was born four years earlier, and since then Ida had miscarried twins and delivered a stillborn. Once more Dad leaned over and whispered in her ear, "No more."

 I only learned recently from my sister Mertice that my middle name, Rae, was a family name - not a given name - of a friend of Mother's. My parents met at a restaurant in Rochester when Rob was a roofing salesman and Ida was a waitress. She had a flirtatious manner and was a very pert, attractive young woman - all five feet of her. Her round, smiling face attracted Rob to her. Dad, a slim, six-foot, handsome man, was fifteen years her senior. As the typically conversational salesman, he soon learned that Seneca Falls was her hometown and told her his was Auburn, just a few miles away, on Routes 5 and 20.

They were married in 1909, and Ida Mae Armstrong became Mrs. Robert Bruce Wallace. After they were married they lived on Post Avenue, then Weddale Avenue. Then they bought and moved in to 82 Hobart Street where they raised the family. Dad continued as a roofing salesman for Certainteed until 1922 when he purchased a warehouse at Child and York Streets in a neighborhood known then as "Dutch town." He started his own business, naming it Great Lakes Paper Corporation, wholesaling roofing and rough paper, incorporating the business in 1925. The "rough paper" designation referred to excelsior, which was the forerunner of plastic peanuts, now used for packaging material. It came in huge bales which were stacked in the warehouse. As I recall, the bales were about 2'x2'x3' and held together with metal straps. The excelsior itself was like thinly sliced wood. It was rough to the touch, and it took a strong man to lift one bale. When I went to the office with Dad, I would go out into the warehouse and climb as high as I could on the piled bales of excelsior. When the Depression hit and people stopped buying roofing, Dad began carrying wholesale lots of toilet paper and cones for ice cream, respectively. It was an incongruous combination of well-selling products.

The picture on the cover of this book is me, chubby and cute, sitting on a child's chair when I was about two. Naturally, I don't recall the picture being taken, but my sister Mertice recalled it clearly. In her own words, "I remember the day that picture was taken of you sitting in the little chair. A photographer came down the street and asked Mother if she wanted some pictures taken. I said, 'Wait a minute; I want to get my doll.' So I ran upstairs to get my favorite doll to have my picture taken holding it, and when I came back outside, the photographer was gone." These words were recorded by me two years before Mertice died. Knowing she remembered things I was too young to recall, I had asked her if she would be willing to have me tape a talk about her youth. When she passed into spirit, two years later, I used some of her own words in her eulogy.

Mertice also recalled that I was chubby with fat cheeks until I was three, and then for the next three years I was sick and became thin. One of those years, I believe I was four, a very high fever made me delirious and I screamed in terror as I saw lions and tigers jump over the foot of the bed at me. I don't know the medical term for the diagnosis, but my sickness was caused by pus in the kidneys. The doctor didn't give Mother much hope. Upon hearing the news when he came home from work that day, Dad raced upstairs. Joy told me many years later that he had never run that fast for her. Sibling rivalry memories linger long. Some memories are sweeter; Mertice told me that when I got better she took me out of my crib and rocked me. "It was my idea, that's all."

Author in her Father's lap with Mother and eight siblings

Author as sailor, 1939. Front row: Alvin, Mother, Ellen Rae, Mertice
Back row: Bruce, Marcia, Blake, Joy, Ada

I have few memories of my father since he died when I was only five years old. I do recall hiding behind our big front mahogany door with glass in the center. It led into a vestibule, similar to a mud room now. Then another door led into the hallway. I would get behind the mahogany door when I heard Dad's car stopping in front. With excited anticipation I waited for him to open the door. Then I would jump out to scare him. It was a grand game. When I was ten months old, the Wall Street crash came and the Great Depression began. Looking back, I'm sure my father believed that if he could keep the company going and weather the Depression, he would be able to build up the business once more. Between the years 1910 and 1926 my parents purchased a dozen properties in the city of Rochester. All except the homestead on Hobart Street and the business at York and Child Streets (on a six-track railroad line) were on the east side of the Genesee River, which runs through the city. Dad had often said that land is the best investment. I can only conjecture that he sold off all the properties one by one, trying to hold on to the home and business properties in the hope that if he could weather the financial storm of the Depression he could build up the business again. In those days a father and husband was seen as the breadwinner and it was shameful for a man not to be able to provide for his family. There were some who committed suicide in those years, unable to face that shame. Dad was under a great deal of financial pressure - the business with no or minimum sales, the mortgage, the expenses of raising nine children.

The fondest and most lasting memory I have of Dad occurred when I was four years old. One day he drove me to the office in a Model T Ford he was very proud of. It was the first car owned on our block. On the way to Great Lakes Paper he was singing "Oh, Dem Golden Slippers." I asked him if that was his favorite song. He said, "One of them; can you name this other favorite of mine?" And he whistled "Camptown Races." At the end of the song we sang the last few words together, "Oh, dooda-day." Mertice told me years later that he also loved "Beautiful Dreamer" and "Drink to Me Only with Thine Eyes." As he pulled up to the curb on Child Street, I opened the car door and, upon spotting a huge rock by the curb, I gleefully said I would jump over it. He warned me not to, but being the spoiled and strong willed child that I was, I jumped. I didn't clear the rock, but landed on it, opening a gash on my left knee which began to bleed profusely. The scar still remains as a reminder of that day when Dad carried me into the office, put some mercurochrome on my knee and bandaged it up.

"I'm going to lie down for a while," Dad said to mother one morning before he left for work. He had never taken a nap at any time of day, much less early in the morning. He never got up. Blake was only 19, but it was his sad task to drive around to the schools to pick up his five siblings, including me. The teachers only informed us that our brother would come to pick us up.

I don't recall the funeral, or seeing Dad's body laid out in the living room. (It was common in those days for the deceased to be "laid out" in the living room of their home.) I was sent to a neighbor's house. Much later I heard that it was the coldest winter on record and the ground was frozen to the point that Dad's burial had to be postponed until spring. Dad was a member of the Masonic Order and had reached the highest degree of the order, Shriner. His fellow members carried the coffin out of the house, down the sidewalk under crossed swords held by other fellow Masons in full dress with plumed hats. It must have been a regal sight indeed. I didn't have a chance to say goodbye, but I'm certain that I missed him. In my child brain I probably thought that he left because he didn't love me. It was the first of four major losses in my young life. The following year my grandmother died. I recall one visit to see her. She lived on a farm outside Seneca Falls. She was a large woman; at least she seemed so to me as a young girl. Her white hair was pulled back in a bun and she wore metal-rimmed glasses. She baked big, soft, molasses cookies which I loved, and would point to the wild chickadees in the bushes outside her kitchen window. She would imitate them, "Chick a dee dee dee." I remember Grandma Armstrong with warm pleasure. Years later when I told this to my sister Joy, she said with an amazed expression "Grandma?" It's strange how each person has a unique memory of others and one's relationship to them, sometimes based on relatively small but significant interactions. The following year my sister Leah was committed to the Rochester State Hospital. But I'm getting ahead of my story.

Mertice told me that none of the other children were at Dad's funeral, but she was taken by a neighbor to the house while Dad was laid out so she could say goodbye to him. I never had that opportunity. Mother was left with five children; the others had married and left home. Marcia, the oldest, married after leaving Cornell when, with the Depression, tuition money ran out. I still have a letter which Dad wrote to her while she was a student at Cornell. Ada, the second oldest, had married a newspaper man at the Democrat Chronicle. I've heard conflicting stories about the financial situation after Dad's death. Joy, seven and a half years older than I, told me that Dad had left $50,000 in life insurance, but Mother continued to live as before, to impress the neighbors. As a result she lost the house to foreclosure. Mertice, six years older than I, told me that Dad left no such amount, because he had borrowed on his life insurance, never dreaming that he would die so young. He had always enjoyed robust health. Mother used to say, "He wasn't sick a day of his life." As a matter of fact, three days before his death his doctor gave him a clear bill of health, suggesting only that Dad cut back on his salt consumption. I think Mother worshipped Dad because

I still recall her referring to him as "a prince among men." Apparently he was a very romantic fellow. Mertice told me that he and mother went to a musical on Broadway in New York City once, taking a train to Albany and a night boat down the Hudson.

It was probably a good thing that Dad died in the winter, during the school year, or I might have missed him more. School kept me busy every day, and I enjoyed learning. I was a curious individual, and have remained so throughout my life. I walked to PS 44, about 15 blocks away. I started kindergarten when I was four, because I would turn five in December. I used to love climbing the huge piles of snow on the curb on the way to school. Up a pile, down to the driveway, up the next one and down - all the way to school. On the way I stopped at Decker's Dairy to buy a half-pint of chocolate milk to drink with my peanut butter sandwich for lunch. There weren't any hot lunches then, just a room where we sat and ate. I still remember my kindergarten teacher, Mrs. Johnson. She was a short, stocky woman with a round, happy face. In the warm weather, as we filed outdoors to the playground, she would say, "Don't touch. Don't touch." It was a confirmation of the behavior existing at home: there was no touching there, either. No hugs, no "I love you." I was never tucked in at night, and never given a goodnight kiss. In view of this, one particular night sticks in my mind. Someone - Mother, a sister? - came in, put another blanket over me and pulled it up under my chin. It was such a special moment. I was a lonely child - and a gullible one! I remember being told, just before Christmas, that the paint specks on the window pane were elves which Santa sent to watch me to see if I was good or bad. I would sit for several minutes trying to see their faces! And a schoolmate told me once that eating the little piece at the end of a banana would kill me! I sometimes still think of it when I peel a banana. I heard a joke at that time: What did the river say when the elephant sat down in it? The answer is "Well I'll be dammed." Swearing was strictly forbidden, at least by the young. My older siblings took great joy in asking me to tell the story, knowing I had to alter it. I said, "Well I'll be darned." And everybody roared with laughter at me.

It was a bleak time during the Depression. Some say the Depression lasted until the beginning of our involvement in World War II, which would be from late 1929 to December 1941, the time of the attack on Pearl Harbor by Japan. Lack of money was the paramount focus; survival was the primary goal of life. No one had any money for anything extra, and there was a struggle just to find money for food. The radio was small consolation, but President Roosevelt's "fireside chats" seemed to cheer the adults. I always wore hand-me-down clothes. There was a red dress I had to wear a long time, until I got the next dress. It took me years to like the color red again. Once in awhile, on a Saturday, I would be given a quarter for the movie at the Arnett Theater and ten cents for candy. Theaters didn't sell candy in the lobby then, but there was a candy store next door. I would sit through two or three showings of the same movie. There were also many cartoons, as well as the Pathé News of current events.

I can also recall that one day when I was six, Ada's husband, Bob, took me to the barber for a haircut. I liked the "boyish bob" the barber gave me, but Mother was furious, saying to Bob, "What have you done to my baby?" When I was nine or ten I was sent out into the neighborhood with a huge box of toilet paper in a cart. I was to sell the rolls to neighbors- 10 rolls for a dollar. Nobody had bills of any kind- what we used to call "folding money." I brought back home pockets full of coins. A card table was set up and all the coins were poured on it, and everybody counted the pennies, nickels, dimes and quarters. I don't recall what the money was spent on, but I suppose it was for food. I remember horse-driven snow plows coming down the sidewalk. You could hear the jingle of the bells on the horses, signaling their approach. And in the summer I recall jumping on the back of the iceman's truck and grabbing a few slivers of ice off the deck left from his chopping the ice into blocks. He chopped out a 25-pound or 50- pound block, grabbed it with large tongs and threw it up onto his shoulder, which was covered with a thick pad to protect his skin and keep the ice from melting. Then he carried the ice into the house and put it in the icebox under which was a tray to catch the melt. The tray had to be emptied frequently because if we forgot to empty it, the kitchen floor became flooded. .

There were other deliveries to the house - the milkman (we used to play "milkman" with a bunch of empty bottles and a carrier), the rubbish collector, and the coal man. A long, metal chute was laid from the coal truck to the basement window and when the driver shoveled the coal onto the chute - wow, what a clatter the pieces of coal made striking and rumbling down the chute. You could hear it from every room in the house. At night the furnace was banked, and as the furnace was stoked up again in the morning there was a grand rush to the favorite heat register to catch the rising heat. The worn spot on the wallpaper about three feet above each register attested to this action.

One day I was sitting on the stoop in front of the house, waiting for someone to bring me an ice cream cone from Love's store on Chili Ave, up on the corner of our street. The ice cream was handed to me with a piece of wax paper over it, to keep it clean. It was a special treat - a nickel cone! One winter day I was entrusted with a dollar bill, to go to the store. I lost it. My sisters and brother took my cart to the spot I indicated, filled the cart with snow and took it back home to melt it. Several trips were made, but the dollar was never found. I felt very bad, but no one punished me. I never got a spanking; nor do I recall any punitive measures against me as a child.

I don't recall any Christmases during those years. They probably did not include a tree and gifts. This was in sharp contrast to the years before, as I heard about them. Dad would set up the tree on Christmas Eve, but leave it undecorated. Santa was the one who decorated the tree and brought the gifts. What a surprise it must have been on Christmas morning, to see the bare tree suddenly alive with lights and balls and tinsel, and lots of new toys and gifts under it. The Christmas morning ritual was that everybody lined up at the top of the stairs, youngest first, and on Dad's okay we came down the stairs to behold our Christmas in the living room. Alvin, four years older than I, reminded me years later how impatient he got, waiting for me - as a toddler - to descend the steps one at a time.

After Dad's death, as the effects of the Depression were felt more and more deeply by Mother, my siblings were sent elsewhere to live. Mertice went to New York City to live with Marcia, our sister. Joy went to live with Uncle Charles in Philadelphia. Alvin went to live with a family in the country. I think I might have been sent to a farm, where I recall collecting and candling eggs. (Candling was a process of holding the egg to a bright light to see if there was a red spot in the yolk, which would signify that the embryo had begun to grow and the egg could not be eaten.) But I didn't stay there, for some reason. I returned home and the only ones remaining with Mother were my sister Leah, and I. Mother didn't - couldn't work. Even if jobs had been available, which they weren't, it was then considered that a woman's place was in the home. In those days there were no social services or social security benefits. After Dad died, Mother turned to drinking. It began to occupy more and more of her time. She became unpredictable in her behavior and her attitude toward me. One day she would be kindly and accepting of my presence, and the next day I would be intolerable to her and she would say, "Go play in the sandbox," or, "Go outside and play." After school it was my task to take a market basket of "empties" to the nearest bar and get full bottles of beer. There weren't any laws then on selling alcohol to children. Or, if there were, the bar owner ignored them.

Attending school was something I truly enjoyed, although I wasn't an honor student. I was a little surprised when I rated 26th in a class of well over 200 at West High. I think one reason I liked school so much was that it was predictable. The same teacher, the same subjects, the same schedule constituted an environment which I knew from one day to the next, unlike my home life in which Mother was always unpredictable. In the cold weather, Mother would spend hours on end sitting in the large, dark living room by the fireplace, gazing at the fire. She pulled down all the window shades. It was a gesture indicating that she wanted to shut out the world. And she did. Drowning her feelings in alcohol became her primary occupation. Later on, Leah began drinking by the fireplace with Mother and stopped spending time with me. Leah had often carried me around the house on her back, to give me a "horseback ride"; she played children's games with me. Then one day she became sullen, pushed me away and didn't want me around anymore. Another rejection of me by a family member! I learned later that Leah's behavior had become increasingly aberrant. One example I heard was that one day she had taken all the pictures off the walls and put them under her bed. On her 17th birthday Leah was particularly sullen and withdrawn and would not even acknowledge the day's occasion. Her behavior became so erratic and frightening that Mother was advised to have her committed. In 1936 Mother signed the papers required by law to commit Leah to the Rochester State Hospital, where she spent the rest of her natural life. Her diagnosis was manic-depressive schizophrenia. Mother's grief over the commitment was severely exacerbated by the fact that mental illness in those days was seen as a serious moral stigma. Leah never got to finish high school. She died on her 72nd birthday and paid for her own funeral with money she earned working in the laundry at Rochester State Hospital - until a law was passed forbidding patients from working. As a teen-ager I went to visit her, and as I walked down the cold cement hallways with barred windows, I used to think, "Please, God, I don't ever want to live in a place like this." There were times I was not allowed to see her; she would be in a manic episode and constrained by a straight jacket. When my own children were young, I would pick her up at the hospital on Sunday and take her home to join our family for dinner. Sometimes she seemed as normal as anyone; other times she would sit silently, staring into space. When tranquilizers were discovered, they evened out her manic-depressive episodes and she no longer had to be placed in a straightjacket.

I was a lonely child. I didn't know how to make friends. I was in a large family and yet after everyone else moved away, leaving me and Leah and Mother in the house, I felt very lonely. I remember reading a poem which appealed to me as it seemed to express my personal situation. The poem was titled *The House With Nobody In It*. Affection was not expressed by Mother and she and I were the only ones left after Leah was committed. Mother distanced herself from me with drinking and I was more frequently told to go outside and play. At that time I began having a dream which became a recurring one for several years. In the dream I came home from school to see my mother hanging clothes in the backyard. Why would such an innocuous dream be recalled - and repeated? It would be many years before I understood the dream. Only in counseling did I address the dream and its meaning. Only after pounding a pillow, crying, and yelling at an image of my Mother, shouting, "Come outside, come out into the sunshine," did the dream stop.

My only respite from the dreary house after school was playing in the sandbox in back of the house, under three lilac trees - two purple and one white one. I made roads and tunnels for tiny toy cars and trucks, the kind known today as "matchbox" cars. I spent many hours in that sandbox. After a rain, the sand molded very nicely to form bridges and buildings for my cars. I was a tomboy and loved to climb the tree by the garage and get on the roof, surveying the neighborhood from on high. I played baseball with the boys who lived on the street. We also played kick-the-can, hide-and-seek and king of the mountain. A girl who lived down the street asked me over to her house. She wanted to "play house," and she handed me a doll. I tossed it the length of the attic! She didn't speak to me after that. To this day I don't know why I did that, but possibly my home life had deteriorated so much that I couldn't comprehend the idea of a good "play house" life - even in make-believe terms. Marbles was another favorite game of mine. I was so good at it that I beat everyone in the neighborhood and my pockets were always full of those multi-colored, beautiful, round prizes I had won.

My otherwise happy school days were marred one day when I was in the second grade. I don't know why, but I did dislike the teacher. I had a very bad habit of talking in school, and she often reprimanded me. One day after telling me to be still, she came to my desk and asked me stand up, which I did. She slapped me across the face. I don't recall that it physically hurt, but I was deeply embarrassed. I told my mother about the incident, and she called the principal of the school. The next day I smirked at the teacher, knowing she had found out I told on her. It's a wonder she didn't kill me that day.

Joyous catch on honeymoon fishing trip, 1949

Kindergarten photo
1935

In the fourth grade I was so excited when the class was introduced to pen and ink. Something about writing with ink seemed very special to me, and I always took very good care of the pen I was entrusted with. Every desk contained an inkwell. It was a small bottle in a hole in the front of the desktop. The bottle had a hinged top. The pens were tapered pieces of wood with replaceable nibs. Everyone was given a pen of their own and a small cloth to wipe off the pen after writing with it. There are other memories of Hobart Street: I got my first new bike, and I rode it for miles in every direction. I learned how to stand on the crossbar (it was a boy's bike) while riding down the road, relishing the great sense of freedom it afforded me. A neighbor named Martin - his last name was Dombroski or Dembrowski, I'm not sure which - lived across the street and was in his twenties. We developed a close friendship as he taught me how to catch fireflies in a jar on warm summer nights. He was more like a brother to me than my own siblings and spent time teaching me how to repair my bike. It was refreshing to have an adult want to spend time with me. Perhaps he too was a lonely person. Those were the years when anyone with a "foreign" name was treated differently.

The Second World War made everyone realize what a small planet we really live on and how interconnected all humanity really is. Foreign names have now become normal in the news, but in those years widespread prejudice was common. Derogatory slang terms were common for Jewish, Polish, Italian immigrants and others. Mother hated Catholics and reminded me to cross the street when I got to the corner where St. Augustine's Church stood. I soon learned that many of my friends were of the Catholic persuasion but I saw no reason to fear or dislike them. My father hated Jews, for reasons unknown to me, but I will speak of this later.

One day there was an accident at the railroad crossing by Dad's office. It was a six-track crossing, and a car had been hit by a fast freight. Martin was the driver and as he drove across the tracks the train smashed into the car. He was killed instantly. I do not know whether there were warning signals where the street crossed the tracks or not. Perhaps the signals were not in working order. Perhaps Martin had been drinking, though I never saw him drinking, much less inebriated. Another dear person gone out of my life; my fourth personal loss in five years. I was 10. Because of the strong impact Martin made on my life, I named my second son Martin in his memory. I tried to locate his parents to tell them so, without success.

I don't recall my brother Blake marrying, nor do I remember his wife, Cora, but during her pregnancy there was a night I will never forget. It was 1938, and I was nine years old. I and three sisters went for a week to a cottage on Skaneateles Lake. Dad had a friend who owned a cottage and in the early years he took the family there for a week's vacation every year. My sister Marcia loved the place so much that she rented the cottage for years after Dad died. It must have been a welcome retreat from the din of Manhattan, where she lived and worked. The cottage was very secluded, on the east side of the lake. It was a mile in any direction to the nearest neighbor. The lake was a mile across at that point, and the sheep farm up the hill behind the cottage was a mile away. The end of the lake was four miles south, with no cottages south of us. The nearest landing was a mile north. The only access to the cottage was by boat or on foot, by a rugged trail. It was a rainy, stormy night at the cottage. The four of us were busying ourselves, playing cards, listening to music, talking, and trying to ignore the fierceness of the weather. I was nine, Marcia was 27 and Joy and Mertice were 17 and 15, respectively. Suddenly, we heard footsteps on the porch. They were slow, foreboding. The fear in the air was tangible. Who could it possibly be? Who would come in this storm to this desolate location to where four females were? Marcia finally screwed up her courage and opened the door. It was Al, our brother. He was only 14 but had been sent from Rochester because there was no one else to send. There was no telephone at the cottage. Al stopped at the last cottage before heading down the trail, to ask for a flashlight. He was refused. He slid on the trail coming in, and nearly fell in the lake twice, but he got to the cottage - to tell us the tragic news: Cora and the baby had both died in childbirth. It was the first funeral I had ever attended. Blake was disconsolate. We grieved mother and child, and we grieved for his grief.

Author and nephew Robert Tuttle at Skaneateles Lake, circa 1939

It was the spring of 1940 when Mother lost the house on Hobart Street to foreclosure. She had met Harry Dodge, an elderly Spanish American War veteran, at the local bar. My mother was an alcoholic, but she was smart. She knew she would lose the house to foreclosure under the prevailing economic circumstances, and she did. Mertice described the day we moved: "Before Mother lost the house at 82 Hobart, she got a loan from Household Finance on the furniture; that kept her going for a few months. When we went to Garfield Street, Household Finance sent a man to collect the furniture. But while he was talking to my mother, my siblings were moving the furniture into a van. Ada laughed about it later - we were moving the furniture he was supposed to be repossessing right out from under his nose and he didn't know it!"

Harry Dodge owned a double house on Garfield Street. Harry asked mother to marry him and I think she saw it as an opportunity to provide housing for herself and her family. In effect, he was her meal ticket. It was a symbiotic relationship - she got a home for herself and her kids plus a drinking companion, and he got a drinking companion in his home so he wouldn't have to make the trip to the neighborhood bar. He treated us all well, but there was no emotional connection between him and us kids. Mom and Harry lived on the first floor, and five of us moved into the second floor - Joy came back home from Philly, Ada, now divorced, returned home; and Mertice and Al came back, too. So we had a home together again. We never were an affectionate family. We cared about each other, but never showed it in any gesture. There was no hugging; feelings were not discussed or expressed. I recall a very comforting sound which I used to hear as I lay in bed at the Garfield home. There was a roundhouse a few blocks away, next door to General Railway Signal (manufacturer of railroad signals). Trains would chug along the tracks into a huge round

21

building and I could hear the steam engine puff and puff, in descending intervals of time and I would lie there, predicting the rhythm of the puffs. It was a very comforting sound and I would fall asleep to it.

In my last year at PS 44, the seventh grade put on a play, "The Courtship of Miles Standish." It was to be in mime and I was asked to read the script - in the wings and out of sight. I was too shy to be on the stage, so it sounded fine to me. I was chosen because I was told I had a strong speaking voice. I was very proud to be in the play. It was a thrilling experience, but I don't recall any family members attending the performance. One of the statements in the play has stuck with me ever since: "There are none so blind as those who *will* not see." Some people, with clear options open to them, see only what the past has brought them and expect only more of the same. Some people are unwilling to look at possibilities and gaze instead on what cannot be done rather than envisioning something that can be done to improve a situation. It is interesting that I vividly recall that line in the play and what it meant to me. And yet, our graduating class took a ride across Lake Ontario on the Colburg (Canada) boat out of Charlotte Harbor. I remember going on the cruise and I enjoyed being on the water all that time, but I don't recall any specifics about the journey.

There were day trips that I was taken on - to Manitou Beach or Grand View Beach, both on Lake Ontario. After swimming we went to Ackerman's hot dog stand on Lyell Avenue. Unique to Rochester at the time was the white (pork) hot. Whenever we had a picnic the person cooking the hotdogs asked, "White or red?" White was my favorite. Letchworth Park in Livingston County was another favorite place. We would picnic by one of the waterfalls and one day we walked onto the railroad trestle which rises about seventy feet above the river. We didn't go across it, just out far enough to look down at the water below. I was young and the view was pretty scary. The longest distance we went for a picnic was Bluff Point, the promontory at the crotch of Y-shaped Keuka Lake. The Wagner mansion was then vacant and we would collect faggots and build a fire for cooking. The view was exquisite; we could see the entire stem of the Y from there. Now the Wagner mansion is restored and occupied by a young family. Recently I went to see the gorgeous view one more time and in spite of the private property signs I approached the house and asked the young mother if I could see the view. She agreed. Then I went down the hill a short distance to see the Garrett Memorial, "the little chapel on the mount" which sets in the forested side of the hill, overlooking one leg of the lake. Today church services are held Sunday mornings at nine in the summer, but other than that, the chapel is closed to the public. After picnicking one time years back, we (Ada, Joy, Mertice, Al and I) went down to the chapel, which was then regularly open to the public. As we filed in Ada, then in her twenties, was forbidden to enter the chapel because she was wearing shorts!

It was in the summer of 1941 that Harry Dodge died, and we had to move out of the house at Garfield Street. It was just one of the many moves I would have to make in the following years. I was too young to know anything about the why of our move. And even if I had understood the reason, children at that time were not encouraged, or even allowed, to speak unless spoken to. Children were to be seen but not heard. Sometimes today I marvel at the freedom children have to question authority. It goes way too far sometimes, but surely children ought to have the option to express their opinion about their surroundings, even if they do not participate in the family decisions. Although I was 12 at the time I don't recall Harry's death or his funeral, nor do I know what became of the house he owned which we all lived in for a little over a year.

.

It was also in 1941 that I graduated from PS 44 and entered West High. That year, because of a change in the districting, all the students of PS 44 were given a choice. I could go to Madison High, then a block east of Genesee Street, or West High, further south facing on Genesee Street. Mertice had attended Madison, but my other siblings all had gone to West. In any event, I chose West High (now Wilson Magnet) and attended five years. I continued to like school. But I had an English teacher, Mrs. Smith, who constantly compared my work to Marcia's, her student eighteen years before! Marcia had been a straight A student and was valedictorian of her class. One day, after I wrote an essay for her, Mrs. Smith said, "Now you sound more like your sister." I recall something else about Mrs. Smith. As I boarded the bus one day to go downtown, I saw her. I was amazed to see this exalted person riding a common bus! I sat next to her and one thing she said that day stayed with me. The exact words elude me, but she said in effect that I had two sides, a pragmatic one and a creative one.

West High graduation, 1946

I favored math and English, disliked history and science subjects. For some behavioral infraction one day in Biology class I was sent to the cloak room for the remainder of the class. Who did the teacher send to let me out but my friend, the smartest girl- indeed the smartest person - in the class (if not the school), Jean Schaefer. We had gone through PS 44 together and then into West High. I always felt inferior to her. She knew the Latin term for every tree. She took several years of Latin and every math course offered. One day she asked me what I thought of reincarnation. I didn't have a clue what the word meant, but unwilling to admit it to her, I said that I really hadn't thought much about it. After high school we lost touch but 56 years later we reconnected when a man from Texas called me in Cohoes, looking for the Ellen Wallace who had graduated from West High in 1946. He was trying to get a 65th reunion together! After he advised me that many of our classmates were now dead, I asked him if Jean was still alive. He said yes, but she had married. He gave me her new name and her telephone number. When I called to ask her if the name Ellen Wallace meant anything to her, to my great surprise she said the name Ellen Rae Wallace did! I was incredulous! But she told me later that she had always called me by my first and middle name. Jean and I continue to have lunch together occasionally, and sometimes wonder how, or if, our lives would have been different had we kept in touch through the years.

I played baseball after school in the eighth and ninth grades. I was a pitcher on the girls' softball team at West High, and a pretty good one too. I still love the game and enjoy baseball season immensely, sometimes watching two games simultaneously on TV, switching channels back and forth. In my sophomore year I took a job at a grocery store which precluded any participation in after-school sports. Geometry was my favorite subject, and I got the highest final exam mark ever in that subject: 89. I had to work for every good mark all through my education. Maybe that is why I value education so much. Or maybe it's because I was raised in a home where education was considered paramount, weighing in far above feelings and their expression. In an age when boys attended college but girls were not so encouraged, Dad considered it essential that Marcia seek a higher education and so enrolled her in Cornell. Unfortunately she did not finish due to the financial restraints of the family in the Depression.

We lived briefly on Post Avenue, and then in the summer of 1941 we moved to Earl Street where it was only a short distance to walk to West High. On December 7 the war began with the attack on Pearl Harbor. On December 8 our principal called a general assembly to hear President Roosevelt's "Day of Infamy" speech over the radio. We heard with horror about the destruction which brought us into WWII. I was only in the eighth grade and did not understand the scope of the consequences. It didn't occur to me that I would be personally affected. Being an underclass student I did not interact with the seniors and so had no idea how they felt or if they understood that upon graduation they would be drafted into the service to fight on foreign soil for American freedoms.

We continued to live on Earl Street until Joy, Mertice and Al got married and left home. During those years I frequently rode my bike to South Park (Genesee Valley Park) which straddles the Genesee River on the south side of Rochester. Having been inspired by my movie idol Sonja Henie, I learned to ice skate backwards on the rink there. And there was the time I went there with two boys I palled around with. We double-dared each other to walk across the river on the catwalk under the bridge across the Genesee. We walked it, but it was scary to look down through the grating to see the river flowing below us. A few years later, Joy and I took our tennis net and our rackets to the courts

27

by the river. In those days we had to string our own net on the court. One time, when I was sixteen, we put a canoe in the river; I still have a picture of me taken by Joy on that trip. The most joyful memory of South Park is of the summer concerts on a Sunday evening. There was a band shell in the park and the Rochester Park Band would play marches and light classical music. For the most part the audience sat on benches up the sloping lawn. We always took a blanket to sit on, and I recall with great pleasure how I truly enjoyed sitting on the ground listening to the music lilt across the warm summer air, and rouse me to stand for the spirited close with "Stars and Stripes Forever." It endeared me to outdoor concerts which later I would come to love at Saratoga Performing Arts Center. I always loved music and when I was in the tenth grade I auditioned for the high school choir. Immediately the music teacher realized I couldn't read music, in spite of my effort not to show it. He confronted me about it and I said no, I couldn't read music. But he accepted me, saying that I had a good strong voice and he would put me next to an alto who could read music and I could follow her. And so it was I sang in the choir for three years. I enjoyed every minute of it, especially singing my favorite, "The Battle Hymn of the Republic." There was a publication at that time which printed the words to all the popular songs. I bought it regularly and memorized the words to all the songs of the day. "I Don't Want to Play in Your Yard," "Polly-wolly-doodle," "Macushla," "A Nightingale Sang in Berkeley Square" are just some of the songs I used to sing. I believe I got the love of music from my older sisters. As a teenager I heard a lot of classical music at home. Music definitely played a role in my youth. Sometimes Mertice played the piano and I would sing "Parade of the Wooden Soldiers" with her. Joy, at one time, fell in love with the music of Gilbert and Sullivan. One of G and S's operettas was "HMS Pinafore," and one of the songs was "Now I am the Ruler of the Queen's Navy." Joy also memorized poetry that she favored. One poem,

"Jabberwocky," from Lewis Carroll's *Through the Looking Glass*, she recited so many times that I too memorized the first few lines.

When my siblings and I were living on Earl Street, my mother lived elsewhere. Because she was preoccupied with alcohol and behaved in radical ways, Ada found Mother a small apartment to live in. One example of Mother's odd behavior is that she once had her telephone listed under six family names. Time after time her drunken behavior led to eviction and Ada would have to find another place for her to live. Although Ada herself drank on weekends she was unwilling to put up with Ida's constant drinking which was always accompanied by complaining and arguing. Ada was what is now commonly known as a "functioning alcoholic."

It was while we lived on Earl Street that we got word from Blake, still in Philadelphia, that he had been drafted into service in the US Army. Later he became what was sardonically known as a "Ninety Day Wonder," having completed an accelerated three month training in Officer's Candidate School (OCS). He was assigned to the 14th Armored Division (tank corps) of the US Army. While in the service he met and married his second wife. After two sons were born, he was sent to France. No one but his wife went to see him ship out of New York. In the meantime, on Earl Street Mertice, Joy and Al all married and moved out. Al left for a job in Buffalo; Ada and I were the only ones left. Ada couldn't afford to pay for the six-room flat on Earl Street for which she and Joy and Mertice had all paid the rent; now Ada had to foot the bill, which she could hardly afford on her income. So we moved to a smaller apartment on Somerset Street. It was while living there that my Uncle Charles came to visit from Philly. He was short and stout, a jovial man who sold cigars for a living. He also liked to drink as he chomped on a cigar. Even though I was now 13, he took me on his lap and told me that I should get

29

my hair curled - a mission he apparently was assigned by Ada. The mission accomplished, I agreed and got my first permanent wave - then with metal curlers attached to a huge, heated machine which provided the curl. It was very uncomfortable, but I liked my new curly hairdo.

We weren't in that apartment long, for whatever reason, and we moved to an apartment on Thurston Road near Ravenwood Avenue, over a grocery store. It was my sixth home in 14 years. I didn't realize it at the time, but Ada had made a personal commitment to herself to see me through high school. In fact, Ada became my surrogate mother. Ada was a binge drinker but also a functioning alcoholic. She worked at a full time job, drinking only on weekends. Nevertheless, whenever we moved, she always found an apartment in the 19th Ward, within West High's district so I didn't have to change schools. Ada was tall and thin, like Marcia, but in her early years she was more athletic. She had auburn hair and dark eyes. She was kind, fair and very generous. It was often said of her that she would give you the shirt off her back - an idiom of the times. Other idioms were "peel me a grape" (based on a song with that title), "so's your old man," "same to you, Buddy," and "go fly a kite."

I now had curly hair, but my teeth were greatly in need of attention. They had always been badly decayed, to the point where I refused to smile and reveal them. While I was in PS 44 I was supposed to go for dental care. I would be given a nickel to take the bus to the Dental Dispensary on Main Street in Rochester. I think the dentists were students of Strong Medical School, but in any event, they didn't use any Novocain, so I was terrified to sit in the chair. I lied to my Mother that I had missed the bus to the Dispensary. Later, when we were on Earl Street, my sisters sent me to a dentist in Pittsford, to whom Marcia had gone. I didn't like the long ride to Pittsford; it required transferring buses downtown, but he was a

30

well known dentist. At 12 I got my first partial plate; my front uppers. Now I could smile. It felt so good to be able to smile that I smiled constantly and I was told to stop grinning all the time. Having very low self-esteem as a child, I didn't make friends easily. But I made some friends on Earl Street, and we would hang out together. After getting my partial plate, I had a Halloween party which included dunking for apples (a Halloween game in which several apples were floated in a tub of water. The object was to grab an apple in your teeth and remove it from the water.) I was not going to participate, hoping no one would notice. But my friends kept after me until I agreed to dunk too. I lunged for an apple and got a grip on it, but suddenly my plate came loose and apple and plate went to the bottom of the tub. Like a flash my hand went down and grabbed the apple with the teeth in it, and I ran out of the room. I was terrified with embarrassment. Only later did I learn that no one knew what had happened.

A boy in the neighborhood went to Aquinas High School. (It has since become coed, but then it was for boys only.) His friends would come and visit on the weekend and hang out with us girls. One night I looked out the window and saw all my friends heading for Eunice's house. They were going to have a party and didn't invite me! I felt betrayed and alone. Afterward I confronted one of my friends and was told that Eunice's mother didn't want me to come. I didn't understand at the time. I was deeply hurt. Only in later years did I comprehend. We were not a "traditional" family, consisting of mother, father and children. I lived with three sisters who frequently entertained their boyfriends overnight. It just wasn't done in those days. So although my friends were faithful, their parents saw me in quite a different light.

Americans, too, were being faithful; the war effort focused on advertising government bonds, and most people invested in them. The government's fear of an attack on our country led to blackouts and wardens being hired to be sure all lights were extinguished. The daily *Democrat and Chronicle* listed the names of the soldiers who had been killed the day before. But families did not learn of their loss through the newspaper. A soldier was assigned to go to the home of the family and when the number reached larger proportions, a telegram was sent to inform the family that a loved one had been killed in action.

In my early years I made an occasional train or auto trip to New York City to visit Marcia and her son Robert. Marcia was tall and thin, with a sophisticated look and way. She was a real beauty. Funny the things we remember. Once I went down to New York in a car, and as we drove down the highway I lay on the back seat and looked up at the sky. The telephone lines rushed by, merging and separating, merging and separating. We used to play games on long rides: count the cows, or count the number of out-of-state plates. Those were the years when the Burma Shave signs dotted the highways. Posted in farmers' fields all over the countryside, they were small red signs with white letters. Five signs, about 100 feet apart, each contained one line of a four line couplet . . . and the obligatory fifth sign advertised Burma Shave, a popular shaving cream. A couple of my favorites were:

AROUND THE CURVE
LICKETY-SPLIT
BEAUTIFUL CAR
WASN'T IT?
BURMA SHAVE

DON'T LOSE YOUR HEAD
TO GAIN A MINUTE
YOU NEED YOUR HEAD
YOUR BRAINS ARE IN IT
BURMA SHAVE

32

The first time I took a train to New York and saw Grand Central Station I thought they had roofed over the world! Marcia had taken a well-paying job as a secretary at a large law firm. I was four years older than Robert and yet I was supposed to baby-sit him when Marcia sent us off to see the current Broadway shows. Robert knew his way around New York like the back of his hand, while I was clueless about the territory. I fell in love with live theatre and still appreciate the great shows I saw then: "Porgy and Bess," "The Red Mill," "Show Boat," "Blossom Time" and others. Marcia also took me to several art museums. She would talk about the various artists, and though I don't remember anything she told me, her enthusiasm for fine art made me appreciate the works of the masters. One day Marcia took me to the Hunt Room at the Waldorf Astoria for my birthday. It was an elegant and exciting experience for me.

Drinking was a given in the household of my childhood. The question, "Do you want a drink? " was never asked. It was always, "What have you got to drink?" The first time I got drunk I was 13. It was just before a trip to New York, and there was no one to take me to the train station except Jack, a friend of the family. He picked me up early, so we stopped at a bar to have a drink, just to kill time until the train departed. Children were not forbidden in bars, nor denied alcohol. I don't know what the drink was, or how many drinks I had, but it was my first time drinking alcohol, so one or two probably made me drunk. Jack wasn't trying to get me drunk, it just seemed to be a given that I would have a drink. We left the bar and he poured me on the Pullman car. I fell asleep for the trip and woke up in New York with a hangover. My headache was awful, but I was afraid to tell Marcia. Later I realized how ludicrous this idea was, since Marcia drank as much as anyone in the family. I still remember her lamenting one time after she moved to a new apartment, that the only drink she had to offer the movers was crème de menthe!

It was while living on Earl Street that I had my first menstrual period. I went to the bathroom and realized I was bleeding. I went to Mertice, then 18, and told her I was dying. She went to the cabinet, handed me a napkin, and said, "It'll happen every month - here, use this." That was the extent of my sex education at home. Hygiene classes, school mates, reading and listening would have to fill me in on the rest.

When Ada and I moved to Thurston Road I was fourteen. I obtained a work permit and got my first job, at Hart's food store, downstairs from our apartment. My pay was $.25 per hour, and by law I could work only 20 hours per week. So I worked every day after school and on Saturday. Next door to the store was an ice cream parlor, and on payday they let me make my own sundae - a real treat! Mr. Dreger was the manager. He was short, large boned and grey-haired. I think I saw him as a father figure. He was fair and honest with me. My job included weighing and packaging sugar and potatoes, weighing and pricing vegetables for customers, helping the cashier bag groceries, and cutting butter. Butter came in 50-pound blocks. It was my job to place a metal frame with strands of wire on top of the butter block, and push down, make one cut, then turn the tool around and push down again, making the other cut. The result was 50 one-pound pieces of butter which then had to be wrapped. One day I had the 50-pound block a little too close to the edge of the counter, and one entire slab fell on the filthy floor of the back room. I was horrified! Fearing that Mr. Dreger would suddenly appear, I quickly picked up the slab, scraped the dirt off each one-pound piece and wrapped them as fast as I could. I hoped that the people who bought the butter would not notice the scrape marks or get sick.

Working at Hart's was a good job at the time, because WWII was on, and it was difficult, if not impossible, to get cigarettes, butter, sugar, and meat. So when these items were delivered to the store, I had first crack at them. Mr. Dreger let me buy them, and Ada appreciated the cigarettes. Another good thing was that one of the store's customers was my geometry teacher, and I was so proud to weigh his produce for him. I think I saw him, too, as a father figure. We lived upstairs over Hart's, and I remember a very funny incident while we lived there. One day Ada decided to make baked beans. She soaked them overnight, and then she came home for lunch and put them on the stove to boil. She told me to check on them every half hour to make sure they did not boil dry. So I went up once, found them cooking nicely, and added a little water. Later I went up and the gas had been turned off. I turned it on again. Later I went up and added some more water; then the next time I went up, the gas was turned off again. I turned it on again. That evening we solved the mystery. Johnny, Ada's boyfriend, had come over, seen the stove on and turned it off. He did that a couple times. Somehow the beans got cooked, but it gave us a laugh for years afterward.

The store had a meat department with a butcher who was a tall, burly red-head. He ran the meat department independently of the grocery department. Mr. Dreger went away for a week-long summer vacation. One of the days he was gone, while the cashier was out to lunch, the butcher came around to the front of his display case and put his hand under my T-shirt, feeling my tiny breasts, which were just beginning to develop. I was angry, hurt, and perplexed by his behavior. I pulled away quickly and never told anyone. When Mr. Dreger returned from vacation, I quit. He asked me why but I would not tell him the reason. It was not the first such offense against me. When we lived on Post Avenue, I went to the candy store for some penny candy. The clerk

35

asked me if I wanted to go behind the counter and pick out my own. I thought it was a grand idea, but as I reached into the case to choose my favorite, he put his hand on my embryonic breasts under my Tshirt. I looked down to see a heavily tattooed arm. I fled, never to enter his store again. I told no one about that, either. It was years before I could see a tattoo without remembering that incident.

My second job was at Strong Memorial Hospital, where sixteen was the minimum age to work. It was good to have a job that paid $.35 per hour! I worked after school and on the weekends. I was a messenger, working with four or five other girls my age. After morning classes at West High, I walked up Genesee Street to Brooks Avenue where there was a drug store on the corner. (I bought a chocolate milkshake with an egg in it. I guess I considered that a good diet.) Then I walked a path between Plymouth Avenue and Genesee Street. The path ended at Elmwood at the entrance to Genesee Valley (South) Park. Then over the bridge to Strong Memorial Hospital. Our job as messengers was to escort patients to their floor upon admission and deliver messages and flowers all over the hospital. It was a very big hospital (as it still is, but today an entire new building stands east of the original hospital). I knew every nook and hallway of it. If my work didn't take me to a certain floor, I would go just to see what was there; one day I was totally surprised when I suddenly came upon the morgue! My coworkers teased and teased me about being a "baby" because I didn't smoke. Wanting so much to be accepted, I learned to smoke, and continued the habit for thirty-nine years.

Since the messenger job required a uniform, I had a locker in the basement of the hospital. One night I went to my locker to find that someone had stolen my clothes, so I had to wear the uniform home on the bus. After about six months of being a messenger, I began working as a ward helper on C2, the women's surgical ward. My job included putting away the linen from the linen cart which arrived from the hospital laundry daily, serving the meal trays, filling the water pitchers twice a day, cleaning the beds every time a patient was discharged, and feeding patients who had had eye surgery. In those days if one eye was operated on, both eyes were bandaged. I hated feeding patients because every one wanted something different. There was a day when 12 people were discharged, so I had to clean and make up 12 beds. When I say clean the beds, I mean every coil of the springs had to be brushed with soap and disinfectant, even if the bed had only been occupied a day or two. The first time I had to set up the food cart with utensils and dishes, I opened a drawer in the kitchen on C2 and jumped back when cockroaches scrambled all over the silverware. I was shocked. A nurse said not to be concerned; it was usual. After that I tapped on the drawer before I opened it.

 There was a patient named Mrs. Thurston, who had been in C2 for years. She was in her forties and had become paralyzed when a box at work fell on her back. Though she would never walk again, she accepted her lot in life and always had a smile. Everyone who met her came to love her. There was another patient, thirty-something, who had been admitted for a surgical procedure. She was epileptic. The day she was discharged, I went in to say goodbye, and shook her hand. As our hands clasped, she went into a seizure. I was powerless to do anything. I knew she couldn't help it, but it was very painful for the few moments when my hand was immobilized in a vise-like grip. When the siezure ended she apologized profusely. Another patient, admitted for brain surgery, took a liking to me and a few days after her surgery she handed me a $20. bill and said, "You and Barbara go out and have a good time."

Barbara was a nurse who had come from Boston to work. She was short and round-faced and with her naturally curly hair and ready smile had a girl-next-door look. In those days every nurse had a cap unique to the nursing school from which she graduated. Barbara's stood out because it was a tiny cap, with frills and a small black band, representing Massachusetts General. Although she was about six years older than I, we hit it off right away. The Head Nurse on C2 was Miss O'Malley, a tall, regal red-head with a take-charge personality.   She took Barbara aside one day and told her that as a professional she should not socialize with a lowly ward helper. We got a great laugh out of that afterward! O'Malley was a strong willed woman who ruled C2 with an iron hand. Her word was law, and her standards were high. Even the doctors respected - or feared - her. She ran a tight ship and wouldn't tolerate anything but excellent work from those who toiled on C2. I picked up on the situation very early on, and tried hard to do the best job I could. As I was putting away the linen one day, O'Malley came to me and said, "How is Ada?" I was shocked to learn that this C2 head nurse had gone to school with my sister! I didn't expect it would garner any special privileges and it didn't.

It was while I was working at Strong Memorial Hospital that President Roosevelt died. It was April 12, 1945. The entire C2 floor was in mourning. In every room I entered I could hear sobs and words of praise for our fallen leader. It was as though everyone had lost their brother. Roosevelt had brought hope to a nation stunned by the Wall Street crash. He implemented many social programs like the Civilian Conservation Corps, the Tennessee Valley Authority and most prominent and all-pervasive, the Social Security program. He was greatly loved by millions, and they had showed their allegiance by voting him into office four times.

Three weeks later we got word that Blake had been killed in action in France. At that time I was living with Mertice in an apartment at the corner of Plymouth

Avenue South and Clarissa Street, next to the bridge. Now it is known as the Ford Street Bridge. Ruth, a woman in the apartment next door, had befriended Mertice. When I came home from work at the hospital one day Ruth came over and blurted out, "Your brother's dead." I couldn't believe her words; I couldn't understand her cold expressionless attitude. I never found out how she knew before I did or why I got the news that way. It was a shocking and painful moment for me. Blake had been drafted while living in Philadelphia. I sincerely hope that somewhere in that city, on a WWII memorial plaque, his name appears: Lt. Charles Blake Wallace. A week later VE day was announced. Two weeks later Blake would have turned 30. He left a wife and three sons. Mertice took it very hard, as she was closer in age to Blake than I and had shared more experiences with him. As with all survivors in time of war the living had to go on the best way they could. Grief was not alleviated by the knowledge that neighbors, friends and coworkers were going through the same grieving process.

My coworker Barbara and I used to go horseback riding at a stable on Lyell Avenue. Once she couldn't meet me at the stable, so I asked Bill, one of the stable workers, if he would ride the trail with me. As we cantered along a hedgerow, suddenly I heard a buzzing in my ear. I shook my head, but it stayed. It would be still, then buzz; be still, then buzz. Bill and I dismounted so he could look in my ear. He lit a match to attract the bug, but to no avail. We went back to the stable and he tried it again. No luck. So I went to St. Mary's Emergency Room. They put mineral oil in my ear and floated it out. The bug was so tiny you could hardly see it. I went to work (I had started an evening job at the *Democrat & Chronicle* proofreading want ads) in my jodhpurs. When I arrived late, my coworkers had a great time kidding me, asking me, "Where's your horse, Ellen?"

There was a time when I mentioned to Barbara that I had had waffles for supper the night before. She said she loved waffles and could she come over some time and have them. So we set a date. She worked the second shift, 3-11PM, so it would be a very late supper. The day before I asked her what she wanted to drink with the waffles. She didn't like wine and I didn't like beer, so we settled for whiskey and ginger ale. I went to the Four Corners liquor store to buy a bottle. I remembered hearing the terms "pint" and "fifth," so in my naïve mind I calculated that a fifth (being a fifth of a quart, I thought) would be smaller than a pint, which is half a quart. Imagine my surprise when the clerk brought out a very tall bottle. I was taken aback, but I didn't think I should ask, so I bought it. As we enjoyed our waffles we made drinks with a single shot, then a double, then half and half whiskey and ginger ale. Even though Barbara was in her twenties, she didn't bring any wisdom to the situation. We were not alone in the apartment; Joy was there. She had moved in for a few weeks with her kids while her husband got settled in a new job in Pennsylvania. We offered her a drink, which she took. She said nothing about our behavior, but left us alone in our folly. We became totally drunk. Barbara went down the stairs to leave, and I followed. I stood in the doorway watching her lean against the street light, and then weave down the street toward the corner where she had to catch a bus home. I went to bed, but the room swam around me, so I called to Joy. She said, "It's a good thing you're home the first time. You'll feel better in the morning. I'll hide the bottle so Ada doesn't find it when she gets home." Only in later years did I realize the strange reasoning of her words. In the first place she was in effect saying that the first drunken episode is a kind of rite of passage which everyone has to experience, and in the second place Ada would likely return home drunk herself.

On May 8, 1945, victory was declared in Europe. There were great celebrations, although fighting was still going on in the Pacific theater of war. I asked Mertice to celebrate with me, but she said she didn't want to. She felt Blake's loss more keenly than I, as she was closer in age and had more memories of him. In 1944, when her husband was shipped overseas by the Air Force, Mertice returned from the base in Biloxi, Mississippi and en route back to Rochester stopped off to visit Blake, who was then stationed at Fort Knox, Kentucky. She told me that he took her to the officer's dance and said she could be escorted by anyone she chose, but she assured him that he was her escort of choice.

On August 6, 1945, the first atomic bomb ever dropped on an enemy killed thousands on Hiroshima. The extent of the devastation was beyond imagination. What had we, as a nation, wrought? I recall people looking at each other wordlessly, in awed response at the magnitude of the deaths and destruction. Thousands upon thousands killed in one horrendous explosion. I think there was a deep sense of shame that our country had inflicted such horror on a population. Then a second atomic bomb was dropped three days later. On the 14th Japan surrendered. Little did we know the full magnitude of the destruction and slaughter. Only in later months and years did we learn of the long-range effects atomic radiation can wreak on the human body. We had destroyed a huge population of civilians in the name of justified war. Yes, the war was over. But what a price was paid in lost lives of the innocent, the suffering of thousands and the shame of our action.

Finally, the war was over. While the men were fighting overseas, thousands of US women had been hired for the various production plants - ammunition factories, auto factories (no automobiles were produced from 1942-1945 due to the US military needs). It was the beginning of women in the workplace. "Rosy the

Riveter" was a popular song. And with all the able-bodied males from ages 18-38 off to war, another popular song, "They're Either too Young or Too Old," hit the radio airwaves, including this refrain:

> They're either too young or too old,
> They're either too gray or too grassy green
> The pickins are poor and the meat is lean,
> What's good is in the army,
> The rest can never harm me.
> (From *Reading Lyrics*, Pantheon Books, 2000.)

In my senior year at West High I attended classes only in the morning. I had already taken most of the required courses to graduate. After classes I walked to the hospital, where I worked from one until seven; then two evenings I worked at the newspaper office on Main Street until the work was done - usually about 10:30 pm or 11:00 pm. I loved to go to the Mayflower Donut shop on Main Street, across from Sibley's department store. Their specialty was waffles with ice cream and chocolate syrup, which I still sometimes enjoy for a decadent breakfast treat.

This busy schedule of school and two jobs ended when I graduated in June, 1946. Ada and I were living in a second floor flat on Henion Street, near Bull's Head. I went to the Senior Ball with a friend's brother with whom I had fallen head over heels in love, though he was 23 and I was 17. We had dated two or three times before, and although Ada frowned on the relationship she didn't bar me from asking him to take me to the Senior Prom which was held at the Starlight Ballroom at the Sheraton Hotel on East Avenue. It was pure heaven to be on the dance floor with Jim, even though I had never learned to dance. He was gracious about it and after the dance he took me home in his pick-up truck. On the way we parked for awhile. I was in love, and that night I shamelessly offered myself to him, but he turned me down. I have been grateful through the years that he did so, but that night I was crushed.

As soon as I finished high school, I decided to seek a job that was more interesting or more challenging. The hospital work had little future and I was weary of its routine. I applied for, and got a job at the *Daily Record*, then and now the legal paper in Rochester. It was a fine job for me at the time. I went to the office, picked up several copies of the day's edition, delivered them to various law offices downtown, and then went to the Plumbing Bureau, the Building Bureau and the Marriage Bureau to collect data for the next day's edition. The Marriage Bureau was in City Hall on Broad Street. (Today City Hall stands at the corner of Fitzhugh and Church Streets.) After lunch I went to the County Clerk's office, where the Daily Record had a typewriter. The office was used by the D&C reporter, as well as two county employees who also typed their work. I spent the afternoon hours typing pertinent information from deeds and mortgages as they were filed out in the County Clerk's office by the lawyers, buyers and sellers. My day ended when the typing was done. Often it was 7:00 PM. Then I took the work I had typed to the office for the typesetters. I was not a good typist - I was a fast typist. But the boss and the typesetters didn't care what the copy looked like as long as they could read what had to be typeset. I loved the job.

A few months after I started that job, Ada called me and asked if I would like to go Miami, Florida with her. She had asked several friends to accompany her, but they all said no. It was the trip she had been planning for years. Now that I was out of school she was free to go. She wanted to get a divorce, and couldn't, in New York State due to what was known as the Enoch Arden law. Only if you'd had no word from your spouse for five years could you be eligible for a divorce, but Bob saw to it that every year he sent a postcard to Ada. I was torn about the invitation. I liked my job very

43

much. I mulled it over in my mind and finally sought advice from a friend who suggested that I probably wouldn't get such an opportunity very often, so I should go. My boss at the *Daily Record* knew a newspaperman who worked for the *Miami Herald*, in Miami, so he wrote me a letter of recommendation. It didn't help, because when I applied in Miami, I was asked to take a typing test, which I failed miserably. Unlike the *Daily Record's* requirements, The *Miami Herald* insisted on rapid typing *plus* accuracy. So I got a job at Jackson Memorial Hospital in Miami, as a ward helper. But I want to tell you about that trip to Miami.

Ada had bought a used car from Mertice's husband, who owned a body shop. I didn't have a license, so Ada had to do all the driving. When we got to Pennsylvania the gas tank was leaking and we had to get a new one. Then in South Carolina we had more car trouble, but soldiers from a nearby military base were hitch-hiking, and got the car going again. As we arrived at Daytona, Florida, the car broke down again. It was towed to a garage. While it was being worked on, a man hanging around the garage asked us if we would like to see the race track while we were there. The Daytona races were run on the sandy shore of Daytona Beach, before the current track was built. We agreed to go with him. Ada sat in the middle and I sat by the door. I wouldn't remember that except for what happened. As we drove down one street, the driver said "This is n_____ town." I was shocked; it wasn't a word I'd been brought up with. Mother had had a Negro woman come to help her with housework once or twice a week and we were taught to respect her. He then reached over and opened the glove compartment. As the door dropped down in front of me I saw a pistol inside. Horrified, I pulled back, and wished I had the option to leave the car. The driver calmly explained that it was necessary to carry one; to "keep them in their place." It was my first taste of Southern, pre-civil rights thinking. Years later Mertice told me about an incident that occurred while she was living in Biloxi, Mississippi, where her husband was stationed at an Air Force base in WWII. A black man and a white man were arguing across the street from the restaurant where she worked. Another white man approached them, pulled out a gun and shot the Negro, killing him. No police car came, no policeman appeared. The next day there was no mention of it in the paper. Mertice asked a coworker about it, and was told, "Oh, that happens every Saturday night."

For miles as we approached Miami, there were hotels and businesses, all with bright neon signs, so we drove into Key West before realizing we had passed through downtown Miami. The first night we stayed in a cheap motel, inspecting the mattress for possible bedbugs. The next day we got an apartment. Ada got a job as a waitress and I started working at Jackson Memorial Hospital because of my experience at Strong Memorial in Rochester. Two months after we arrived I got homesick and wanted to return to Rochester. I don't know why - I had no home to go to. But our living consisted of working and spending time in local bars. I knew that wasn't the kind of life I wanted to continue living, so in early December I told Ada I wanted to go back to Rochester. She put me on a train to New York City. As the train approached Hollywood, Florida, I remembered doing some heavy petting at a party while drunk, and in my naivete I feared that I might have gotten pregnant. I didn't want to chance it. I didn't want to risk the blacklisting for being pregnant out of wedlock, as they said then. I felt safer returning to Miami, believing that if I were pregnant Ada would stand by me. So I got off the train at Hollywood and called Ada to come and pick me up. It sounds strange today with the current mores of society, but in those days a girl was totally condemned by family and society for being single and pregnant. Ada, though perplexed at my decision but forever supportive of me, drove me back to Miami where I stayed until I had my next menstrual period. Then, in January, I boarded a train for New York City and stayed the trip. Twenty-six hours on a coach. It would be 30 years before I boarded a train again. I stopped en route to visit Marcia in New York. She was recovering from a radical mastectomy, and asked me to stay with her. She offered to send me to college. Her employer continued to pay her and she could afford it. I went to Columbia and Hunter. Both told me I would need some classes to become eligible, which discouraged me. Further education at that time just didn't appeal to me, and so I told Marcia I wanted to go back to Rochester. In hindsight I realize that she wanted me to be there for her, with her, in her recovery. But I was too young to sense her need or respond to it. I journeyed on to Rochester. Of course there was no one and no place awaiting me. I rented a room, eating all my meals out. I interviewed for a job at Hawkeye, a facility of Kodak. The job was key-punch operator. Before computers were developed all information had to be punched into 3x5 cards, then the cards were fed into a computer for processing. Kodak sent me for three weeks of paid training, and then I began working. I sat at a keypunch machine in a huge room with about 100 other operators on 100 keypunch machines. It was such a very noisy room it made me feel like a machine myself. I had to punch a time clock four times a day: morning, out to lunch, back from lunch, out at the end of the day. After the job at the *Daily Record*, this seemed too restrictive for me, and I quit after three weeks of work. But before I left, I was given quite a tongue-lashing by the supervisor for quitting "after all the money we spent to train you."

Then I got a job as a bookkeeper on Gibbs Street in downtown Rochester next door to the Eastman Theater. It was while working there that the prejudice my father expressed toward Jews came to the fore. Mr. Hart was my boss, but to my knowledge he was unrelated to the founder of the Hart's food store chain in Rochester. At lunch-time one day I was chatting with my coworker, Edna. I can still see us standing at the office window, looking out over Gibbs Street, and whatever the conversation was, I found myself saying, "I would never work for a Jew." Edna suddenly turned to face me and said, "What do you think Mr. Hart is?" In one quick instant, I realized that prejudice is an empty, unreasoning, unfounded judgment call against a person we could not even identify. It was a profound lesson, and I am grateful that I learned it when I was young.

I loved the job, but I was very unhappy living alone in a room. I called Joy, who now lived with her family in Brighton, by the Genesee River. It was known as West Brighton to differentiate it from the rest of Brighton which was an upscale neighborhood. We met for lunch and I asked her if I could move in with them. She tried hard to discourage me. The roof leaked, they were carrying water and she could only offer me a tiny bedroom. To top it all off, there was no bus service from there to Rochester. She relented and I moved in with her, her husband Gerard, and their three children: Jean, Paul (Buddy) and Ruth. We got along fine. I found someone in the neighborhood to give me a ride to and from work. But I had to take a course in bookkeeping to keep my job. So two nights a week I would stay in town and attend Monroe High night school. The only bus available traveled out Scottsville Road, across the river, so I got off at the railroad tracks and walked across them and back down River Road home. Every night I dreaded the walk across the trestle, not seeing but hearing the rushing water below. I consoled myself that it would only be for a few months. As I look at the bridge today, it is only about 70 feet long, but it seemed like a mile then.

Those three years I lived with Joy and her family were good for me. Everyone got along. - Joy, her husband, my nephew, Paul, and two nieces, Jean and Ruth. All accepted me as part of the family. I taught my niece, Jean, how to tie her shoelaces, which she reminded me of years later. There were other experiences

47

during those years which are memorable. Since there was no bus service into Rochester, I had to find transportation to work. A young, married man in the neighborhood offered to give me a ride to and from work. They had a baby and one day they asked if I would baby-sit for them. Since I never paid for the transportation I didn't feel that I could say no, so I agreed. Yet I was terrified because I didn't know anything about babies. Joy assured me that all I would have to do is give the baby a bottle and maybe change a diaper; besides I could call her if I had any problem. When it was time to give the baby the bottle, I prepared it as per Joy's instructions - I thought. However, when I put the nipple in the baby's mouth he just spit it out and kept crying. I called Joy and she said did you take the cap off the bottle before putting the nipple on? Oh, oh, that was it! After that everything went all right.

 Joy liked politics and when the presidential elections began in 1948 she took an avid interest in the race. She got me interested, too, and when the early returns started coming in, we watched the results on TV. I had made a $10. even-odds bet with a co-worker, Irma, that Harry Truman would beat Thomas Dewey. She told me, as she made the bet that she only bet on a sure thing. All through election night - we stayed up until about 4:00 am - we watched the race go one way, then the other. When I left for work, Dewey was ahead and when I arrived at the office, I expected to pay off the debt. Instead, Irma handed me a ten-dollar bill. I said, "Dewey won, didn't he?" And she said, "No, Truman did." It was the sweetest and only ten dollar bet I ever won. Irma's sure thing just didn't materialize, and it seemed to actually pain her to pay off the wager. It is a pretty well-known fact that one major newspaper distributed thousands of copies of the morning paper that day erroneously proclaiming "Dewey Wins." President Truman had his picture taken, holding up that front page, with a huge grin on his face. That, too, circulated widely across the country.

Joy and I were both curious about many things, we both were realistic thinkers and I could talk to her about anything. One time she was reading about the universe and demonstrated to her husband and me the various distances between the planets. The sun, moon and planets were various fruits that she placed on the living room floor, then out in the kitchen. Then she explained their inter-relationship in space. I recall that Pluto was out in the back yard somewhere. It was an introduction to the subject for me, and I relished her enthusiasm for the lesson. It was while living with Joy's family that I met my future husband. I had asked Joy if there were any eligible bachelors in the area. One day she pointed out Steve, walking down the street from the corner store. In his brown denim work clothes he look very dingy and dirty, so I asked Joy what kind of work Steve did and she said that he was an ironworker. His appearance in dirty work clothes did not appeal to me in any way, so I said to her, "Forget him."

Chapter 2: Marriage and Family

1949-1972; Age 20 - 43

Shortly after that first glimpse of Steve in his work clothes, he came to the house one evening and asked me if I wanted to go to the driving range with him. He had never played golf in his life, I found out later, but I guess he saw it as something we could do together. We dated several times in the ensuing weeks. He had been dating a neighborhood woman who was attractive but rather obese. Later on, I heard that she had told someone, "He had to get a smaller woman or a bigger boat." He owned a rowboat and we would go rowing on the Genesee River nearby. He recited Omar Khayyam:

> "Ah, Love! could you and I with Fate conspire
> To grasp this sorry Scheme of Things entire,
> Would not we shatter it to bits - and then
> Re-mould it nearer to the Heart's Desire?"

> "Here with a Loaf of Bread beneath the Bough,
> A Flask of Wine, A Book of Verse - and Thou
> Beside me singing in the Wilderness -
> And Wilderness is Paradise enow."

Although Steve was 16 years my senior, he believed that sex should be saved for marriage. He was conservative, dependable, hard working and faithful. The fact that he drove a fifteen-year-old Model A Ford should have been a clue to his frugality. I fell in love with him, or maybe I just loved the way he treated me. He was the first guy I met who did not expect to have sex right away. We talked and spent time together. He took a trip to see his grandmother in Binghamton and I missed him. When he returned, I told him so. A few months later he wanted to visit his grandmother again and asked me to join him. It would require an overnight but he assured me that we would get two rooms at the hotel. Joy said the neighbors would be very suspicious and upon our return would start counting the months. We disappointed them. Soon after that, we went out for dinner one night. Sitting side by side in a booth, he held my hand as we waited to be served. He slipped the friendship ring off and put another ring on. As I brought my hand up to see, there was a brilliantly sparkling diamond in a Tiffany setting. There was a tiny diamond on either side. I learned later that the setting was platinum. I showed it off at home and at work, enjoying the reflected glow as I moved it in the light.

We began planning the wedding, but from the beginning, Steve assumed that I would move in with him, his mother and grandmother. Although his grandmother and I came to care for each other, his mother was a different story. She liked the lady Steve had been dating and resented my being in his life. In fact, our personalities were diametrically opposed. Once, when we had been visiting with her, as Steve went out ahead of me, she turned to me and said, "You're taking my baby away from me." I was astonished. Her "baby" was 35 and I was 20! Where we would live became a point of contention. We had been attending the First Presbyterian Church, on Plymouth Avenue North in Rochester and both of us liked and respected the pastor, Rev. Murray Cayley. Steve suggested that we take the problem to Rev. Cayley and he would abide by his decision. As you may have guessed, Cayley quoted Scripture: *And he answered and said unto them, Have ye not read, that he which made them at the beginning made them male and female, And said, For this cause shall a man leave his father and mother, and shall cleave to his wife; and they twain shall be one flesh? . . . Mark 10:8*

Steve kept his promise to abide by Rev. Cayley's judgment, and we began looking for our first home

51

together. Our wedding was a small, simple affair. My wedding dress was designed and sewn by my sister Mertice, who was my matron of honor. She was an excellent seamstress and I was delighted that she wanted to do this for me. It rained that June 25, 1949, and I was late arriving at the church. Steve had chosen the wedding music, a song titled Ich liebe Dich ("I love you"). He didn't say it in all the years of our marriage, and neither did I, but he said it that day in music. I was late to my own wedding, late enough so that I'm sure everyone was quite weary of the melody by the time I arrived. The reception was held at Joy and Gerard's home. It was a small, happy gathering, unhampered by the fact that three pails were located in the hallway because of the leaking roof. We honeymooned on Canandaigua Lake in a mobile home which sat on a lot Steve purchased before World War II. Before I met him he had served in the US Army as a combat engineer, serving in five major campaigns, including D-day and the Battle of the Bulge. A combat engineer's task is to check terrain for land mines before the soldiers move forward into the field. However, through all that he returned unscathed.

Wedding day, June 25, 1949
Gordon Gay, best man and Mertice, matron of honor

While we were on our honeymoon Steve wanted to go fishing, one of his favorite hobbies. It was something he really enjoyed and I was willing to learn. After rowing to the southern end of the lake and fishing in the West River, he caught a few bass, and then I got a good bite. I pulled up the line to see what prize was on my hook, and there was a huge mud turtle. Steve said it would make good turtle soup. I wasn't sure if he was kidding, but I quickly told him that he could take the turtle back with him - or take me! I had forgotten the picture was ever taken, but as I gathered pictures to put in this book I came across a snapshot of me standing in the rowboat, holding aloft a fish I had caught on that honeymoon fishing trip. My pride at the accomplishment is clearly visible in the photo.

As we rowed back, a storm came across the lake. It was the first time I had seen a storm approach across a body of water, and it was a lovely sight to see. However, its beauty was overshadowed by the threat it posed to us in the small boat. As the wind whipped the waves higher and higher, Steve rowed fast and hard for shore. Quickly he turned the boat over, and we found shelter under it until the storm subsided.

After the honeymoon, we rented a small home close to his family - the neighbors called it "the doll house" because it was small. But it was sufficient for us. A few days after we set up housekeeping there was an electrical blackout, so we went to bed, as might be expected of newlyweds. As we began to make love, the landlord knocked on the door and called out, "Do you need a candle?" We laughed so hard we postponed our love-making a while. I don't recall just why we left that cozy home, but we moved into a cottage a couple of miles away, right on the bank of the Genesee River. It, too, was quite small. A tiny bedroom and kitchen and a living room only a little larger. It was adequate for the two of us, but when I became pregnant we knew we had to move again, to accommodate the new baby.

It was 1950, the year in which the Genesee River rose to flood stage. We could hear rushing water under the cottage, a frightening sound. After putting the furniture up a few inches, we abandoned our home. Steve stayed with his family and I took a hotel room in Rochester. After a few days Steve called and said he had *shoveled* most of the mud! I dreaded returning to the mess, but that was all we had. The furniture was dry and the refrigerator motor on the bottom had some mud on it, but it ran better than ever after the flood. We cleaned up and moved back in, but immediately began looking for a home to buy.

It didn't take me long to realize that Steve wanted to live close to his family, but the area was in a flood plain and no bank would hold a mortgage on homes there. I was still working at the *Democrat and Chronicle*, proofreading the want ads and I saw an ad for a house on Ballantyne Road. Joy worked at the D&C too, so that night we went with a flashlight to peak in the windows of the house. It was one and a half stories, and seemed adequate. It was too far out of the city to be called the suburbs, and there was no bus service from Rochester, but the neighborhood was well developed with several streets in the area.

We made an offer and bought the house, happy to find an attorney who would hold the mortgage. The flood had caused extensive damage in the region, but it just so happened that in 1949 construction was begun on the Mount Morris dam, near Mt. Morris. They called it the best town by a dam site. Steve got a job tying rods. It's one of the things ironworkers do, besides work on high steel. Tying rods means to fasten iron rods with metal wire, which fortifies the cement poured over them. It was a long job, of course, with long hours. Steve worked seven tens - seven days at ten hours per day. The timing was perfect for us, as we had to come up with $1,000. for the one-third down payment. Yes, the house cost only $3,000. A journeyman ironworker earned a fine union rate, so our income then, added to the mustering out pay he had saved from the Army discharge, enabled us to buy the house. I loved the large front yard, about 200 feet from the road. Along the road was a hedge of wild roses and near the house was a fir tree, about 30 feet high. It seemed to give a great stability to the site. Next to the pine tree was a wild rose bush which bloomed every year at the end of June. We called it the graduation bush. The house needed work - insulation and flooring on the second floor. Steve, in his frugal nature, one day spotted some old pine flooring in the local dump. We hauled them home and stacked them in the front yard. My task was to pull all the nails out and take as much tarpaper off as I could; the rest would come off with a floor sander. I had decided to stay home and be a housewife after the wedding, so I had a lot of time for that dirty, laborious task.

My pregnancy, as with all later ones, was very easy for me. Please do not think that I consider any delivery easy. Labor pains are sharp and painful, but by easy I mean that the total labor time was short. From first to last, my labor pains lasted only three or four hours. I felt better when I was pregnant than at any other time, probably because I took good care of myself, for the baby's sake. Our first child made a liar out of the doctor and me. The doctor predicted a November 13 birth and I, excited about calculating the due date, came up with November 15. When Steve got up on the 14th I told him I was having some pain. He said it was probably gas and left for work. But at 10:00 am, I called Joy and she took me to the hospital. Steve was sent for and came for the birth. Evaline Ann was born on November 14, 1950, at 1:30 pm. Not only did she have all the necessary toes and fingers, but she was perfect in face and form - she was gorgeous! I hadn't had any experience with newborns so I thought all newborns were gorgeous. It would be far beyond my ability to describe the feeling when a child - especially

56

the first one - is put into your arms. For me, a flood of feelings included fear, self-doubt, responsibility, and yet they were all superseded by the exquisite joy of the moment, not to mention the joy of knowing the nine long months were over, and my stomach was flat again. We hadn't decided yet on a name, even when Evie was two days old. Those were the days when a woman stayed hospitalized for several days after delivery. On the second day Steve came to visit and I asked him what his grandmother's first name was. He said Evaline. I thought the world of her. She reminded me of my own grandmother. When we were coping with the issue of living with his family, Grandma had had a stroke and when I went to the hospital to visit her she told me you and Steve need your own home. The baby was named Evaline Ann. We called her Evie for short, which she still prefers.

I decided to nurse Evie, as Joy, who had nursed all her children, recommended. However, after four weeks Evie was crying after her feeding, so I asked the pediatrician about it. He sampled my breast milk and determined that although I provided quantity, the milk was like water, with no nutrition. So I went to formula. One day, when Evie was only a few weeks old, the oil-fired floor furnace backed up and soot filled the house. I retreated to the bathroom with the baby, but the soot even seeped into that room. Evie and I had to escape to a neighbor's house while Steve worked on the furnace. I was very self-conscious about nursing in front of a stranger, but my neighbor, unaware of it, did not offer me a private corner for the task. It was good to go back home, but cleaning up the house was a major job which took many hours.

We loved caring for Evie, savoring all the firsts of her growth - first smile, first tooth, first word, first step, etc. I still recall the thrill of seeing her standing for the first time, when I went in one morning to get her out of her crib. Steve enjoyed Evie as much as I. One day I saw him standing next to the changing table where he was diapering Evie. He was holding his hand inside his shirt, Napoleon style. I asked him what he was doing, and he said, "Warming up her diaper before I put it on." One day when I had put Evie out in the yard to play, inside a fenced area, I looked out every now and then to check on her toddling activity. One time I looked out and couldn't see her. I rushed out to check the fence to make sure there wasn't a way she could get under it. I was frantic, because I couldn't see her at all. Then I spotted her, lying down in the shallow culvert next to the neighbor's fence, fast asleep. Of course, she was taking her afternoon nap. Perhaps that experience set her future - she has always loved being outdoors.

Without Joy's help I don't know what I would have done those early months of Evie's life. Joy taught me how to bathe, feed and care for Evie. I think Joy enjoyed teaching me what she had learned from Bruce's wife, years before. Steve was easy to cook for, which made my housewife tasks simpler. He never complained about the food. Not even the day I decided to clean out the refrigerator and found a fish in the freezer which had been there for some time. I decided to fry it for Steve, though I didn't care for fish myself. He had caught it and frozen it. When I put it before him, he said nothing, got up and threw it away. Then he said, "Have you got any eggs?" I asked him what was wrong and he told me the fish had not been cleaned! What did I know? I thought it was funny the eyes were intact, but I had seen sardines in a can and thought that was okay.

Even after the lessons learned from Joy about mothering, she and I saw each other often. Because of our upbringing we both liked to drink. She was a good mother and didn't drink during the week, but on the weekends she would have a few drinks. I drank very little in those years. I was quite content to take care of the children and the house. Steve was not a social person so we rarely visited friends. On one Saturday evening Joy and I went out together to have a few drinks, and on the way home, as we approached the Elmwood Avenue bridge, I said to her, "I always wondered what it would be like to drive my Volkswagen down this foot path in South Park." I turned onto the path and drove down along the river. Suddenly we saw a couple lying on a blanket just off the path. They looked up in horrified amazement to see a car approaching. We continued on and as we came to the merry-go-round, up on a knoll, I decided to return to the park road. I made three passes before I negotiated the knoll, but then we continued home.

I drove Volkswagens for twenty years, after falling in love at first sight of my first VW in 1961. The first one was a 1959 model and had a rod (which I never used) by the front bumper for crank-starting the engine. There was no gas gauge on the dashboard. When you ran out of gas, you reached down to the floorboard by the pedals and turned a lever which meant you had one gallon left. It worked fine for me until the day I reached down to turn the lever and it had already been turned!

In late 1951 I became pregnant with our second child. I wanted our children close together, either because I was ambitious, (raising little ones is a lot of work and vigilance) or because Joy had hers close together. Or perhaps it was because pregnancy and birth were uncomplicated for me. I was truly blessed in that regard. I never suffered morning sickness and had no problems except the discomfort of backaches which always attends the last few days from the heavy load. Roy was due on June 30, but that date came and went. Desperate for the delivery and extremely uncomfortable with the record heat that year, I begged the doctor to induce labor. He prescribed castor oil and quinine. He explained the castor oil was to "clean me out" and the quinine would trigger birth. No one has ever explained why quinine could trigger birth, but it did. And so, on the following Saturday night the labor pains began and I went to the hospital. Roy Stewart was put in my arms on July 13, 1952, and my first words were, "My God, look at that nose!" It seemed to take up most of his face! (Though as an adult it does not have such a prominent appearance). I think I had just been spoiled with Evie's perfect looks. In the years to follow he exhibited good looks without an over-large nose. The local newspaper visited a Rochester hospital occasionally and took pictures of all the nursery babies. Roy was there when they came to Strong Memorial Hospital, and I received a photograph of him as a newborn.

Parenting took on a new dimension with two babies, but I loved them and I loved playing with them. One fun thing I did was to lay them down on the living room rug and put a page of newspaper on top of them. They would kick and swing their arms and giggle at the crinkling paper. Of course they got pretty dirty with printer's ink, but it was worth it. Babies are very washable. Steve and I had decided on three children as a nice family, and so I became pregnant again. But the house was pretty full with four of us, and we needed more space, so we decided to add on to the house. Originally the house was about 24 feet by 24 feet. We doubled the space in six months - ourselves. We designed the rooms, adding two small bedrooms and a living room. We did have the digging done for the foundation. The walls would be cement blocks. We decided to make our own, purchasing a block-making machine and cement mixer at Sears & Roebuck. Steve told me how to use the cement mixer and what mixture of cement, sand and water to use. Typical of my nature, I set up a schedule to make 20 blocks per day. The cement mixture had to be put into the block machine to form it. Then each block, on its pallet, had to be carefully placed on the ground to "season" - it took about 24 hours for the soft cement to harden so the blocks could be stacked. One day, after I had set out the 20 blocks on pallets and proudly scanned my accomplishment, our cat, Fubar, jumped on top of one of the blocks and it slumped into a pile of soft cement. When it slumped, it frightened her and she jumped again - landing smack on top of another block, which then slumped. She kept jumping, and the blocks kept slumping. I could only stand there in amazed anger watching her as she ruined nearly a day's work. She quickly disappeared, which was what probably saved her life that day. The name Fubar, Steve explained, was an army term meaning 'fouled up beyond all recognition'. I suspect the F stood for another word, though. The two of us built the entire addition, with Steve even doing the electrical wiring and plumbing. Steve got some technical assistance from a neighbor, but only the installation of the living room picture window and the furnace were contracted out. We broke ground in June and moved in before Christmas. In early December, when I was seven months pregnant, I laid a brand new hardwood floor, but it was almost fun, after installing the used hard pine flooring we had laid upstairs.

In November of 1953, we got word that my sister Marcia had died in the tuberculosis sanitarium at Saranac Lake. In her recovery from the 1946 radical mastectomy she had contracted tuberculosis and was advised to go to Saranac for treatment. Her son, Robert, moved to Saranac also, so he could be near her while he completed high school. Four of us made the trip to visit her at Saranac Sanitarium - Joy, Mertice and her husband and I. Arrangements were made to have Marcia's body shipped to Rochester where she was laid out at a local funeral home, then buried next to our beloved father. Marcia was only 43 years old.

The company had taken care of all her expenses throughout her illness, a very generous offer for a business. She must have made a deep impression on the legal firm she worked for. Everyone had to take turns for the viewing hours at the funeral home. I was assigned certain times. I said I couldn't do it, but was told by my sisters that everyone had to do their share. I was due in February so I searched and finally found a subdued maternity smock to wear. Being as shy as I was, I disliked the idea of greeting perfect strangers. On my assigned hours, a woman came in who obviously knew the entire family, but I had never seen her before. She began asking me about Ada, Bruce, Blake, Leah, Joy, Mertice and Al. I was trying very hard to concentrate on my answers so as to give her an accurate update on the whereabouts of all my siblings. Then she said, and how about Marcia? I said, "Oh, she's right here!" She gave me a look that would melt a rock. I will never forget that faux pas, but in retrospect, it still makes me laugh. As for Marcia's furniture and belongings, Joy and Mertice went to White Plains to take care of them. They decided that I could have an overstuffed chair with embroidered upholstery and a mahogany secretary. They would dress up our new addition very nicely, when it was finished.

As for my own house where Steve and I were building the addition, I tried to think of ways to keep the children busy, so I decided to build a sandbox. I had good childhood memories of spending many happy hours in one myself. So I ordered the lumber and put together a sandbox six feet square. Since I had to nail the bottom to the sides, when I finished the job, it was necessary to turn the sandbox over. Its weight was too much for me to lift, at least in my pregnant condition, so I had to wait until Steve came home from work. He chuckled as he righted it. The next day a yard of sand was dumped into the box and Evie and Roy jumped eagerly into it, with their collection of tiny cars and trucks.

Unlike today, the sex of the expected child could only be guessed at, and part of the joy at birth was to find out whether the child was a boy or girl. It made it a little difficult to buy baby clothes, because then the tradition was pink for girls, blue for boys. Some people still apply the rule. Before disposable diapers, cloth diapers were used and diaper services flourished, to provide pick up and delivery of clean diapers on a regular basis. A diaper delivery service gift certificate made a great baby shower gift, and brought welcome relief to the new mother. For the shower for my third pregnancy I received a most welcome gift certificate for diaper service. I knew the third child would increase my task of raising a family. Like the previous pregnancy, I went full term and beyond, but Dr. Ekas was adamant in withholding an inducing prescription until two weeks after the due date. So late in February I filled the script for castor oil and quinine, and Martin Wallace was born on the 28th of February. His original due date was Valentine's Day. He weighed in at nine and a half pounds!

One summer, in the late 1950s, when polio was rampant, Evie complained of leg pains, headache and tiredness; symptoms associated with polio. I was frantic with concern. We were at the cottage at Canandaigua at the time, but the doctor vacationing nearby told me to see our regular physician, so I drove to Rochester with her. I was very thankful to God that it was not polio. The next year Dr. Salk developed the polio vaccine, which provided a great protection from the disease that struck so many, including President Franklin D. Roosevelt.

Raising babies and keeping the house was a full time job. I look back on those hectic years and wonder how I did it, but when we are young, we have a great deal of energy. The children had accidents - a fact of which I am not proud. Most mothers will admit that try as we may, accidents come suddenly and we can't always foresee them. But my children's accidents - at least some of them - can only be chalked up to my own negligence or lack of thoughtfulness. When Marty was only weeks old, I set him up in an overstuffed chair in the living room. Although someone told me that drinking beer makes good milk for a nursing mother, I was happy to have a cup of coffee. I put the coffee on the table next to the chair on which I planned to nurse him, and went to get a diaper for burping. In that moment I was away, his tiny hand swung up and touched the saucer, tipping over the cup of hot coffee on him. I rushed him to the doctor, feeling a deep and abiding guilt. He was all right, thank God, with some tender care by the emergency doctor. Later, when Marty was about three, he fell downstairs, putting a deep gash under his arm, which bled profusely. Wrapping him in a blanket and calling Joy to watch the other two, I took him to the emergency room. They took stitches and as Marty healed physically, I healed emotionally. I tried so hard to be a good parent, but somehow things happen which we don't foresee. It is a fearsome responsibility to raise one other human being, and the responsibility increases with numbers. Children bring the greatest joy, the deepest anguish, and the highest pride to those of us who make such a choice. We do our best, but fall short at times.

We loved holidays and birthdays. One year I hid one of the Easter baskets in the dryer, which had the children all stumped until I give them clues. One day as I was washing clothes, I removed some from the dryer and closed the door. As I did so I was singing "Se Magnafique" from a recently released movie *Can-Can*. When I sang *Je t'adore* Evie suddenly quipped, "You just did Mommie." Little moments like that endeared me to the mothering role.

Evie had a terrible accident, at my hand, when she was about four. Foolishly, I let her stand on a stool and watch me do the wash. The machine was old, with a wringer. When I turned to reach for something, she imitated me by feeding the clothes into the wringer, but her hand got caught in it. My God, what had I done! In my anguished guilt I rushed her to the Emergency Room. I don't remember whom I got to watch the other children. I was so distressed and so ashamed of myself. Dr. McCormack told me that she would need a skin transplant; that he would take the donor piece for the grafting from high on her buttocks so it wouldn't show later when she wore a bathing suit. How she would look in a bathing suit years later was the last thing on my mind at the time. The surgery was a success, but left a scar. Whenever I see the scar on Evie, although it is inside her arm, I think of my inexcusable negligence.

For the most part we Douglases were a healthy family. Except for chicken pox, which hit the boys worse than the girls, there were no childhood diseases. On the other hand, I believe when I was a child I had contracted all the childhood diseases. I even have a vague recollection of homes being quarantined when someone was contagious. When the first day of school came, I walked Evie up the driveway to the road and asked her if she wanted me to walk to school with her, figuring she would say yes. But she turned and said, "No, Mommy, I'm going alone." I watched her walk down the road, and I stood there crying. It was a new stage in my life as a parent. At that time we lived on a paved county road, so the traffic was light. Later it became a state highway and the traffic increased greatly. One by one, utilities were installed. The well we used, which fortunately never gave us a problem - it was under the house - was replaced by city water. Sewers were installed and although we were promised that the rose hedge which ran alongside the road would be replanted, it was not.

From 1953 to 1960, I worked in the Transit Department of Security Trust Company, a bank at Main and Water Street. It was an evening job, sorting checks that had to be sent back to the originating bank. After work, I drank with one of my coworkers, and even on Christmas Eve one year, I remember going to a bar to drink after work because I knew Steve's mother would be at our home for the holiday and I didn't want to be there. Actually, my drinking was beginning to get out of hand and it probably was just an excuse not to go home.

In October of 1955, when the children were one and a half, three and nearly five years old, I had a serious accident. It was while I was working evenings at Security Trust Company, sometimes coming home at midnight. I would waken in the morning, after Steve had left for work, and hear the children chattering in their cribs. One night I made French fries for supper and left the deep-fryer with the oil in it, on the stove overnight. Suddenly I awoke to Evie's scream, "There's a fire in the kitchen!" I ran to the kitchen to find the oil was on fire. Somehow the burner was lit under it. I got the kids all safely in their beds and told them to stay there. I actually stood looking at the fire shooting up toward the ceiling and analyzed what I should do! There is an expression "Analysis leads to paralysis." I thought of extinguishing it with a blanket or rug, but opted instead to carry it out the front door to dispose of it. It might have worked, but there was a breeze on that mild October morning, and the breeze caught the flame and blew it into my face. I spilled the oil on myself, dropped the pan and ran to the empty lot next door, rolling on the ground to put myself out, believing that I was on fire. I screamed and neighbors came running. Somehow I got over to the porch steps and told a neighbor to please check on the kids. Joy was called and came over immediately. I asked her if a person could die from burns. I was in shock and shouldn't have smoked, but I asked a neighbor for a cigarette as I awaited the ambulance. Never did a sound seem so sweet to me as that siren's wail indicating that I was being rushed to the emergency room which would care for me. To this day when I hear sirens I pray for the victims and the rescuers, thanking God that someone is getting the attention they need. In the emergency room, they wouldn't sedate me, though I asked them to. When they cleaned the gravel and dirt from the bottom of my feet, it actually tickled. The last thing I remember before passing out in the ER was a cadre of doctors surrounding me wearing white masks on their faces.

Twenty-four hours later I woke up in a hospital bed with both arms and both legs straight out and bandaged. I looked over at a nurse sitting nearby and asked her what she was doing there. She said, "Can you scratch your nose?" I said, "No." She asked me if I could feed myself. I said, "No." She said, "That's why I'm here." Soon I asked for a bedpan. When I had used it, the nurse said, "You'll make it now, your kidneys are working." Only then did I realize that my life had hung in the balance for 24 hours! Joy took care of all my kids, along with her six children, while I remained in the hospital for seven weeks. I can't even imagine how she did it, but God love her for her generous support. Steve never missed a night to visit me. I made two trips to surgery for debridement - a procedure which entails scraping the scabs off the burned area. Both times I was given nitrous oxide (laughing gas) I laughed so hard in surgery the second time that one doctor said, "Next time we'll knock her out." Both times when I awoke from debridement I had excruciating pain. As a nurse handed me a tiny white pill, I recall my deadly serious comment, "Do you think that tiny pill will take care of all this pain?" She said, "Yes," and she was right.

 The doctor told me that if I had had the accident 20 years earlier, I would have been a helpless cripple, but during WWII, when burned pilots had to wait until they got back to a base hospital for skin grafting, it was learned that skin grafting is best done several days after the event because the graft takes better. One day the doctor told me that he expected I would need six grafting surgeries. When Steve came to see me that night I bawled like a baby.

But soon afterward the doctor said he might be able to accomplish all the grafting in two operations. So, the first time he took three slices of very thin skin (I think it was 1/1,000th of an inch thick) off my right thigh to graft onto my arm. Soon after, in the second operation, he took another three slices off my left thigh for grafting onto my feet. The doctor told me that, despite the thinness of the grafted skin, the donor side would always look different from my normal skin. He recommended protecting it in the sun as the donor side is prone to easy sunburn. When I got home in early November I still had some bandages to change daily. Joy brought the kids back to me, but they only stood in the doorway of the living room, staring at me, afraid to come to me. It broke my heart that they seemed to have forgotten me, but it was the bandaging that frightened them so. Finally, they got accustomed to me again. Al's wife, Anne, came over that Thanksgiving and fixed an entire meal for her family and mine. After seven weeks in the hospital, it took another seven weeks to recuperate. It was a grand feeling the first time I got behind the wheel of a car again. .

In 1956 Steve's grandmother, Evie's namesake, died. Evie, only five, was shattered and confused. In my own grief I tried to console her. Steve's mother remained at their home until she retired and moved to Florida to live with a friend. It was never suggested that she move in with us. Steve knew that his mother and I were not close. Evie was in school now, and somehow I wanted one more child, but Steve was adamant. Finally, he acquiesced and I became pregnant for the last time. Again I was late. The baby was due July 30, but July 30 came and went and still no delivery. On July 28th I drove with a friend who lived in Newark, NY to the Mormon Pageant, an annual affair in Palmyra where Joseph Smith founded the Church of Latter Day Saints. Construction was underway during the trip and my friend feared that I would deliver en route. I don't know why she was so worried; she had had seven kids herself so she would have known what to do.

The hot summer continued and I became very uncomfortable as I once again went beyond the due date on the calendar. Once more, I begged the doctor for relief with an induced labor. But true to form he made me wait. However, this time he yielded to my pleas and prescribed castor oil and quinine in only eleven days instead of two weeks. The prescription was to be taken on August 9. I was joyous and confident. After having gone this route twice before, I predicted when the labor pains would begin, when I would go to the hospital and when I would deliver. But it didn't happen that way at all. At the expected time, I took a shower in preparation for the trip to the hospital, but as I got out of the shower, I had a showing of blood. This was a brand new experience for me. I yelled to Steve to call the doctor, as I went into the bedroom to dress, but as I stood there, ready to put on my maternity slacks, I could feel the head start to come. I lay down, hoping that if I were still the baby would wait. Steve called a woman in the neighborhood, Marge. As it happened, Marge's aunt was visiting and she had done some midwifery, so they both came over. Marge's aunt delivered my fourth child and second girl, but did not cut the cord because the doctor was on his way. As I was taken by stretcher through the living room, it seemed like the entire neighborhood was there watching. Later I heard that stories had circulated in the neighborhood about various places in the house where I had given birth! When we arrived at the hospital - because I had to have some stitches taken - the baby was put in isolation, away from the other babies, because she was considered contaminated! The doctor told me later that when a baby comes suddenly, there is rarely a problem. Unfortunately, when Wendy was born I was not aware of that fact.

On the third day of my new baby girl's life, I was struggling to name her. A nurse came in and said, "Haven't you named that baby yet? Why don't you call her Wendy - she flew by herself!" I knew she was referring to Wendy in Peter Pan. I thought about it, though. Wendy Jean. Yes, if Steve liked it, that was it. And he did. Only when Wendy was a mother herself did she ask where I got the name. I told her, hoping it wouldn't make her upset. Instead, she said she loved telling the story to others. When she asked me what significant event occurred the year she was born, I told her it was the year in which President Eisenhower sent US troops to Little Rock, Arkansas, to quell the race riots precipitated by school integration mandated by the US Supreme Court.

When the children were young, winters were sparse, because Steve worked fewer hours in the bitter cold weather. Now there are huge tarps that shelter outdoor jobs, and I think that improves the situation. But we had some winters with little income. I remember one February when Steve worked only two days. He wasn't one to sit around, though. One time he set pins in a local bowling alley just to make a few dollars. Most bowling alleys were automated by then, but there were a couple which were not. I found a parttime job in a bank in downtown Rochester and worked evenings, an excellent time for me because we didn't need to hire a baby sitter. Steve was content to stay home evenings and my income helped to make ends meet. One year everyone in the family developed a boil - on a leg, or on an arm. The boils came to a head, and we healed up. Except Steve. The boil on his leg became infected and he came down with a fever. I called Dr. Schnabel, an excellent family doctor who had been a surgeon in Germany. He still made house calls when most doctors would not. As soon as he took Steve's temperature he told me to get him to the hospital immediately. Steve's body had developed a general infection, septicemia. For four days the hospital doctors tried to reduce his fever, without success. Finally on the fifth day it dropped and Steve came home, but only after losing 10 pounds and becoming quite weak. But it didn't take him long to bounce back and return to work. While he was in the hospital, I had a baby sitter stay with the children one afternoon so I could visit him. When I got back home I had to turn around and take Evie to the emergency room. Her foot was bleeding because a playmate had gashed it with a small pickaxe. I rushed off to Strong Memorial Emergency Department where the doctor took some stitches.

In 1962 the Cuban crisis was created by Communist Russia, which sent ships to that country, and Kennedy enforced a Cuban blockade. They were tense days in the White House as the country anxiously awaited the outcome, but Russia backed down and the crisis ended. That was also the year that Wendy began school. When she was in kindergarten the teacher decided to put on a show with the little ones. I don't recall the entire show, but Wendy played the part of a vamp, complete with lipstick, heels, and swinging a purse as she walked across the stage. Everyone screamed with laughter. But later on, I found out that Wendy had not expected that response. She thought it was a serious part. During her year in kindergarten, Wendy was diagnosed with a "lazy eye" which could be corrected with surgery. The procedure was successful, and Wendy took it like a trooper, as they used to say.

At various times the children chose activities to take part in. The boys wanted to join the Cub Scouts, so I outfitted them from head to foot. Three weeks later, they decided scouting was not for them. Wendy took bagpipe lessons for a while. I was ecstatic because I love bagpipe music, probably because of my Scottish heritage. However, a few weeks later she lost interest in that. It takes a year to study without using the bag; I think that fact rather discouraged her. Evie took up the drums, and marched in the Memorial Day parade one year, playing a bass drum, which she could hardly see around. Someone near me said, "Who is that little girl with that big drum?" I proudly claimed her. Marty decided on trumpet lessons and continued them for over a year.

While the kids were in school I became active in the PTA, and was elected vice- president. I was in line for the position of president the following year, but an overly-ambitious parent had her eye on the job, so I did not contend for the title. One year the girls' baseball coach became ill and asked me to fill in for her. During the few days I coached, one of the girls was hit by a ball and I had to take her to emergency, where she was found to be all right, much to my relief. And, along with the regretted accidents, various interests in scouting, music, and school activities, there were some other memorable times. One spring day I was up on the roof for some reason; possibly repairing a couple of shingles. I didn't have a problem going up the ladder (only about 15 feet), but when it was time to descend I got a little scared. While I was up there our next door neighbor, Myrtle, came over and told me that Fubar, our cat, was dead under her rose bush. The children were in school, so I climbed down the ladder, dug a hole in the back lot we owned, and buried her. That evening I left for work. Steve's habit was to sit in a chaise lounge in the front yard and read the paper after work. Shortly after I left for work, Evie came running into the yard with a cat in her arms, shouting to Steve, "Fubar's alive! Fubar's alive!" Steve realized that I had in fact buried someone else's cat, and he laughed so hard he nearly fell out of the chair. I never did find out whose cat I buried.

To complete this story, we need to jump ahead about five years. We were all preparing to leave for work and school one autumn morning. Evie came running into the house with Fubar, literally coming apart. I got a box to put this suffering animal in and told Evie she could go to the vet with me. When we got there, the vet said it was too late. I asked him if he could take care of the body. He said yes and I gave him the $10. fee. Evie was crying her little heart out. I let her do so for awhile; she was so attached to that dear pet of hers. But then I said I was going to take her to school. She rebelled, saying she wouldn't, couldn't go. I explained to her that if I took her home she would probably cry all day and that wouldn't be healthy; it could make her sick to her stomach. She finally agreed to go. After I dropped her at school, I had to pass by the house to go to work. Roy was home with a bad cold, so I decided to stop to see if he needed anything to get him through the day. As I entered the living room, I noticed a light on in the far bedroom. I went to turn it off and there on the bed was - Fubar! I said to Roy, "Why, Fubar is right here!" And he said, "So what Mom?" I said, "I just paid $10. to bury her!" He laughed and laughed. Again, I never learned the ownership of the cat. Needless to say my coworkers at that time had great sport in ribbing me about my inability to identify my own cat and burying other people's cats without informing them. I have told my black cat story over and over - to friends and from the pulpit.

As the boys got old enough to play what I had once played, cowboys and Indians, I took them to the store to buy guns and holsters. To my amazement, and later gratitude, they both declined. I figured this was a new generation, and not all kids were falling into the old stereotypes. As Roy and Marty got older, their interest turned to motorcycles, which did not please me at all. Marty was into mechanics and one Christmas I bought him an old Volkswagen motor to tinker with. Both boys had a cycle, and I prayed constantly for their safety, but didn't want to interfere with their new love. One day, at sixteen, Roy had an accident. After flipping off his cycle while driving down a dirt road, he scraped along the ground on his face. I was called to the ER, where he held my hand as his face was injected with Novocain and more than a hundred stitches had to be taken. He held my hand so tightly I thought it would break. I had to turn away so I could not see the stitching or the Novocain injections put in his face. We left the ER for our cottage at Canandaigua, to join the rest of the family. When we arrived Marty took one look at his brother's bandaged face and realized what can happen in a cycle accident. I think it was a wake-up call for him to be very careful on his own motorcycle.

Marty and Roy were both popular with the girls. One night at the supper table there was a phone call for Marty. He decided to go upstairs to his bedroom to take the call. When he returned to the dinner table I said, "How did you make out?" He said, "Mom, how can you 'make out' on the phone?" Then there was the time when I asked Wendy if Marty had found a pick-up yet, and she retorted, "Mom, Marty's not like that." I said, "I mean a truck - he's looking for a pick-up truck!" These were all reminders to me of the "generation gap."

In 1962, when all the children were in school, I wanted to work days instead of evenings. I was a good cook, I think, but I didn't particularly enjoy it, and housecleaning and laundry were simply necessary tasks which I found boring, repetitive and unrewarding. I had wanted to go back to work sooner, but Steve asked me to wait until the kids were all in school. Working would mean that I would need to have a car of my own. One day I saw a used Volkswagen for sale and it was love at first sight! Volkswagens were just beginning to arrive in the US. I had to cash bonds to buy the vehicle but it was a romance that lasted 20 years. I recall driving down Lake Avenue, exchanging enthusiastic waves with other VW drivers. It was an unspoken camaraderie! However, my sister Joy derided me for buying a car which was manufactured in a country which was our enemy in WWII and responsible for killing our brother. I was unable in my own mind to make the connection. I felt it was the leadership of Germany which led to the war, not the people of Germany. Through the years I owned a black, white, red, green, blue and yellow Volkswagen, respectively. The last bug I owned was a brand new yellow Volkswagen, but I lost it through my bankruptcy proceedings years later.

Even though I wanted to work outside the home, I was anxious to be home after school with the children. So I sought and found a part time bookkeeping job at the Kodak Executive Garage on State Street, from 10:00 AM to 2:00 PM. The hours were perfect at the time, but after a year or so I longed for a job with more of a challenge. By 1963 we had paid off the original mortgage on the Ballantyne Road house, plus a home improvement loan which we had obtained to build the addition. Steve wasn't much concerned about more building; he was satisfied with everything just as it was. I thought about building a "dream house." Then I thought about building a cottage on the Canandaigua Lake property where we had spent our honeymoon. The property was not on the lake front, but rather we shared about 150 feet of frontage with other cottages in Newaygo Cove. We received estimates and finally had a no-frills, one-and- a- half story cottage put up. I didn't want to have two homes to clean, so we requested four frame walls, unfinished inside. The town office sent a representative to advise us where we could place the outhouse and where we had to dig the well, since the lot was located in a watershed.

Except for the basic kitchen appliances, the room was a living room. We took most of our meals outdoors. Upstairs the children put down sleeping bags unless they could find an empty cot. Before we built the cottage we stayed a couple weeks on the lot, but I was unwilling to deal with camping while the children were still in diapers. The word was put out that we could use furniture others were disposing of and we gathered about four couches and several chairs. After a few months we decided to move one of the couches downstairs. As my sons and nephews tilted the couch to descend the stairs, nuts in the bottom of it which the squirrels had stored through the winter, rolled out of the bottom. The more they tilted it, the more nuts came tumbling down the steps. We all laughed so hard I feared the kids would drop the couch mid-stairs, but they didn't.

Sometime around early 1963 I longed for a more satisfying job than just keeping the books for the wealthy executives at Kodak. I applied for a full time bookkeeping job at Empire Mutual Insurance Company which had a branch office in Rochester and a home office in New York City. It was a challenging and interesting job that paid well. I was in charge of accounts receivable, supervising six people. Later they sent me to New York and trained me to start up and supervise a new accounts payable department. I worked there for five years, leaving only to take a civil service job with New York State Department of Taxation and Finance. I took the exam for it while at Empire Mutual. During those five years I was sent to the home office in New York three different times. I stayed at the newly built hotel next door to Lincoln Center (now the Julliard School). On my first business trip I missed the plane because I was having a cup of coffee at the airport with Joy. All of a sudden, she said, "I think that's your flight!" We ran out, and the pilot was waved at to stop, but he refused and I had to take the next flight. It was a local flight, which traveled over the Finger Lakes, so it was delightful. But I arrived an hour late for my appointment, since my luggage went to another airport and first I had to pick it up before attending the meeting in Manhattan. Fortunately, I was not fired.

I wasn't happy just working days. I wanted to become a CPA more than anything, so, in 1962, with Steve's approval, I enrolled in the BS program for an accounting degree at Rochester Institute of Technology. The campus was downtown, on Plymouth Avenue, but a new campus was under construction in Henrietta, just a mile from our home. I took an accounting major, attending classes three nights per week. My ability to work and attend classes as well as raise a family was tested during the first semester. An additional stress was added when, on the way out of the house one winter evening, I slipped on the porch steps and broke my left wrist. I drove to emergency to have it set and missed classes that night. My hand was hanging at an awkward angle but in spite of that the young ER intern said, "What makes you think it's broken?" I sarcastically retorted, "I guess I'm psychic." I didn't let the cast slow me down. I continued to work, drive and attend RIT.

I was the token female in all the business courses at RIT where many men were returning to evening school as adults. One night, in class - I think it was Organization and Management - the instructor was speaking of women in business. He said that he heard of a woman being a vice president of a company and added, "Can you imagine a woman being a vice president of a company?" It was beyond his comprehension, and if memory serves me, the mostly male class agreed. Stunned at the comment, I remained silent.

In an attempt to save time and money I scratched for every credit hour at RIT. I took a college proficiency exam for a cost accounting course. It was inexpensive and took two hours. I felt I could pass it since I had done some mail-order studying of accounting. I did pass it and gleefully heard that I had earned the three credit hours. The only course I failed was Oral Communications - public speaking. I just didn't have the self-confidence to speak in front of my peers. I heard about a correspondence course in Public Speaking being offered by SUNY Brockport, so I enrolled. All the lessons were mailed to me and all the results were mailed back. I thought I would probably have to take an oral exam as a final exam, but would deal with that when it came. At the end of all the lessons, I was mailed a final exam to be taken on faith at home. I mailed the results and they awarded me the three credits. I never did give a talk in person! I have told this story many times for laughs. I doubt that SUNY Brockport still offers it. Though my transcript shows, correctly, that I had been on probation once, I graduated from RIT with a BS degree in accounting in 1970.

During my first semester at RIT, Danny, Ada's husband, called from New York City. Ada had died from the cancer for which she endured a radical mastectomy five years earlier. I had gone to Miami to visit her after the surgery, elected by my sisters to be the one to go because I was emotionally closest to Ada. So they had chipped in for the airfare. It was pre-jet times and the propeller-driven flight took seven noisy hours. When I went to see Abie (her nickname for Ada Beth) the doctor called me aside and told me that they didn't get all the cancer cells. It was tragic news to take back home. When I heard she was in the New York hospital I knew she was near the end of her life, but I couldn't see myself making the flight with a broken arm. For years I regretted that decision. Two weeks later I was motoring down with my broken arm to bury her. Danny put the funeral off for several days so we could all arrange to get sitters for our children and drive to New York. Danny was Jewish; but his family loved Ada dearly and they helped him arrange to have a Rabbi offer a service that would meet the religious needs of both families. Ada was buried in a Jewish cemetery on Long Island. The car trip from Manhattan to Long Island that day seemed endless. Ours was the only hearse with flowers (against Jewish tradition). For the first time in my life, I saw a waiting line of hearses at a cemetery gate. At the gravesite, the Rabbi spoke in Hebrew. Danny, who had been drinking from a flask, said loudly, "Talk in English, we don't know what the hell you're saying."

Ada's death was my greatest loss; she was like a mother to me, and I loved her deeply. It was the only time, before or since, that I ever had had a sick headache. Al's wife had some smelling salts in her purse, which revived me. When we got back to Ada and Dan's apartment, I was still sick and had to lie down. Finally, we got on the road for Rochester; two cars made the trip, deciding not to follow each other. On the NY Thruway, as we made our way back home, we decided to stop for a meal. We got off the Thruway, drove into a small town and found a restaurant. When we walked in, there were the rest of the mourners from the other car! I believe it was a miracle because we needed each other at the time; Joy maintained it was just a coincidence.

One might say that my life was now in high gear: With a husband, four children, a home, a full time job and night school, I was living an insane schedule. In effect I was trying to do what I wanted most and raise a family, too. I didn't have much time for the kids, but thought since they were busy with their schooling and extra-curricular activities, they didn't need me. They seemed to be taking it in stride because I didn't disrupt their personal schedules. Except for Wendy, who was only five. It broke my heart when she would sometimes say to me as I left for class, "Mommy, do you have to go?" I saw my efforts as being for the good of the family. Steve, being much older, would be retiring while the children were still in school, and only by earning a business degree could I hope to earn an income even close to the good union wages which he brought home. In later years I would say that I did many things then, but I didn't do any of them well. Our marriage suffered, I wasn't there for the kids, and I wasn't that good a student. My drinking escalated as I tried to keep pace with my hectic schedule.

In 1965 Mother died. She had been transferred from Iola Sanitarium for tuberculosis to Rochester State Hospital, on Elmwood Avenue. I didn't know why nor did I question the decision. It is likely that the doctors at Iola were sick and tired of Ida signing herself out for a drinking binge and coming back. This erratic behavior was probably frowned upon. Mother's behavior had been erratic for years. Today I think she might have been diagnosed as bi-polar, which can be treated with medications that were not then available. Also, I'm sure she had no health insurance of any kind, so without a clear diagnosis of TB she probably never got a complete medical checkup.

Not long after she was admitted at RSH - about a year later - she became quite ill. It might have been congestive heart failure. I was with her when she took her last breath. She was 75. Because I hadn't been emotionally close to her, I counted my tears - only two. Then I called Joy to let her know. Ida was buried next to her beloved husband in Mt. Hope Cemetery. Even though her alcoholism kept me at a distance emotionally, I still recall some things Mother taught me, for which I am very grateful. She taught me to respect my elders, she did not swear (unless she was on a binge), she taught me table manners and she taught me to be kind to strangers. She quoted Tennyson's "Come Not, When I Am Dead." "And may there be no moaning on the bar when I put out to sea," which became "at the bar" to the family - a humorous reminder of the time Ida spent in bars during her widowed life. Mother's life and mine were quite different. But Mother, like me, knew the joys of parenting, then destitute years. We both were afflicted with the disease of alcoholism. I was blessed with a recovery program which was just beginning to form when she was increasing her tolerance for the drug.

I don't remember seeing mother read the Bible, but she must have taken Bible study classes in her youth because a jingle to help her remember the first four books of the New Testament was, "Matthew, Mark, Luke, and John. Hold the pig 'til I get on." One of her favorite Bible quotes was *what is man, that thou art mindful of him?* (Psalm 8:4), which to me indicates a deep desire on her part to know the meaning of life. In my adult years I have come to realize the things which she taught me before alcohol overtook her life. She taught me not to speak with a mouthful of food, to honor older people, to be honest, to respect others, to do a task well and to take education seriously. Mother had a great sense of humor. During a series of questions by a young intern, in evaluating her health prior to a gall bladder operation while at Iola, one of the questions (unthinkingly put by the doctor) was, "Are you pregnant?" Her immediate response was, "If I am you can prepare for the Second Coming!"

During the same decade that marked my mother's death, an accident with my Volkswagen in the late '60s brought home a poignant example of my lethargy about the civil rights movement. I was backing out of the driveway at home and the lady across the street was backing out of her driveway. I was focused on an appointment at the dentist, and she was concentrating on a visit to her lawyer. We both looked up and down the road like efficient drivers, but failed to see each other backing into a collision. Since the motor of a Volkswagen is in the rear, my engine was pushed into the body of my car. Her car sustained little damage and she continued to drive it, whereas mine needed extensive work. Fortunately no one was hurt. This incident would not still be in my memory but for the social unrest of the time. It was the year of the racial riots all across America. Rochester was no exception. The National Guard was called out; my auto mechanic was in the National Guard, so for six weeks I was without my own car. It is with shame that I admit I was more concerned about my transportation dilemma than I was about the social upheaval in the country. No buses into Rochester served our area, so I had to beg rides from friends and neighbors to get to my daily job.

But cars brought the least of my problems. In 1968 Evie was scheduled to sing in an All-county Chorus for a community concert. She was very excited about it, and of course, I was looking forward to attending. But

81

a few hours before she was to leave, she complained about pains in her lower abdomen. I gave her something for the pain, but it persisted, and then worsened. I took her to Emergency where doctors did an internal examination, then another. They were attempting to discern if it was her appendix or a mid-menses problem. They wanted to do a third exam, but I said No way. I told them to go ahead with surgery. They told me afterward that they had removed her appendix just in time or her appendix would have burst. Only recently Evie reminded me about how angry she became when the ER doctor asked her if she were pregnant. She told me what the doctor said and I also had become enraged. In hindsight I suppose it was a needful question, but I couldn't imagine my innocent daughter being pregnant. Our memories of the outcome are different, also. Evie recalls that post-op she couldn't participate in the leaping required of cheer leaders, and I recall her disappointment at not making the concert.

In 1970 I started working as a Tax Examiner at the Rochester District Office of the NYS Dept. of Taxation and Finance. It was the same year that my marriage began to unravel. Steve and I never did have a good communication system in our marriage. Our talks centered on the kids, the house, the finances, but we never spoke of feelings or expressed them. I recall a time when I put my arms around him from behind, as he sat in a chair. He immediately assumed that I wanted to make love, which I didn't at that moment. His idea of affection was only as a prelude to having sex, it seemed. Our marriage deteriorated as I continued to drink, not at home but with coworkers. Throughout my years attending RIT my drinking continued and increased.

I called Jack, a family friend, for advice about my failing marriage. I saw his marriage as very secure. Unfortunately it was not, and as we shared our problems and consoled each other for another couple of dates, we became involved in a sexual relationship. About a year into it, one night Jack said that I should go to psychiatric emergency. To this day I don't know why he said it. I refused, but when I got home I realized he was right. He agreed to go with me. I was evaluated, given a prescription for Elavil (a tranquilizer then called a mood elevator), and an appointment for the following week. At the appointment I was interviewed by three doctors who suggested I participate in group therapy. I agreed but I didn't attend the first group and requested individual therapy instead. The therapist was an ex-psychiatric nurse who gave me some real hope. Her counseling was invaluable. I had sought psychiatric help twice before, over the issue of latent homosexuality. Once when I was seventeen and once shortly after marriage, when I was given the Rorschach ink-blot test. Both times I was told that I was normal and did not need psychiatric treatment. I saw the counselor several times in the next few months, who said two things I still recall. She told me that in spite of my childhood experiences I was doing very well, and she thought my biggest problem was my low self-esteem. Her comments did not make me feel better about myself but somehow they gave me hope. Here was someone who acknowledged me as a person worth hearing and talking to. It made a positive and lasting impact on me.

One evening in the spring of 1969 I went to class for the final exam in Biology after drinking and taking Elavil (a combination which could have been deadly). I sat staring at the exam paper, asking myself what I was doing there. I thought I should just get up and leave, but something kept me glued to my seat. I needed a decent mark, as I had cut all the labs in which creatures were dissected. I just couldn't bring myself to participate in dissections. I wrote the test, fearing the worst. A few days earlier I had a dreamed that I got a 36 on the exam. Six weeks later the marks were posted. My mark was 63, barely passing.

In January of 1971, Roy told me that he was joining the Navy. His father supported the decision; I was apprehensive; the war in Viet Nam was raging. Roy didn't tell me until years later that he joined because he didn't want to go to war and he expected Nam to be a land war. When he finished boot training, we went to see him graduate at Great Lakes Training Center: Marty, Wendy and me. When Roy had been in the Navy a few months, he was offered the opportunity to sign up for service in Reykjavik, Iceland, to serve at the NATO base there; he jumped at it. Only volunteers were sent to that base. The three of us took him to McGuire AFB to fly to Iceland. He loved that country, and served there for over three years, completing his four year commitment in the US Navy. He seldom wrote, but once his letter said that spinal meningitis was going around the base! It was as though he was telling us everyone had a bad cold. I stiffened in fear that he would contract it, but he did not. We telephoned him twice, during the holidays. Evie went to Iceland to visit him while she was at SUNY Buffalo. He stayed in Reykjavik for three years, then took ship to Liverpool. It was his first trip on a boat and he was sea-sick all the way. He then hitch-hiked south, almost reaching Marrakesh. He had saved all his leave time so he could see some of Europe when he was discharged, and he did. When he ran out of money, he went back to Liverpool and flew home.

By late 1971 I knew that I was going to leave the home I had established with Steve. For the next few months I announced my plan and asked Marty, 16, and Wendy, 14, if they wanted to go with me. They both said No, which was a blessing because I would barely be able to make it on my own, in my mental state. Evie was attending SUNY Buffalo and Roy was in the Navy. In retrospect, it is impossible to figure out what my thoughts were. But I know I did not value myself, was ashamed of cheating on Steve who had always been faithful to me, did not believe I deserved a home and family. No one ever confronted me about my drinking habits. My family of birth wouldn't, of course, because they drank too. Steve never said anything because he had no experience with alcoholism. And even after I left him, he thought I would return someday because, he told a mutual friend, she'll never make it on her own. Drinking makes one feel guilty and then the guilt takes one back to the drink. It is a deadly syndrome. There is a saying "The man takes a drink, then the drink takes a drink and then the drink takes the man." I am not suggesting that my children caused my alcoholism. By birth, I had that predisposition - but as my kids reached puberty and began growing into their own individuality, I felt diminished by their growing self-awareness. I think I felt overwhelmed by the fact I was surrounded by others with a growing sense of themselves. My children had been my joy when they were small, but now they were coming into their own, so to speak, identifying their own needs, wants and aspirations; expressing their uniquely individual personalities. Whatever the situation and whatever the reasons, I walked out on my family and my home in the spring of 1972, at the age of 43, after almost 23 years of marriage; a marriage that I often said would never end on my account, because I took very seriously the vow of "Till death do us part." I packed my Volkswagen with my clothes and books, and left unceremoniously. It was the first day of April, 1972. It was truly an April Fool's Day - for me, not Steve. I was totally unaware of what lay ahead for me, and unwilling to know.

Chapter 3: The Interim Period

1972-1977; Age 43-48

Nineteen seventy-two was the year of the Watergate scandal and the resignation of Richard Nixon. Both events were the result of unprecedented investigative journalism and the operation of an informant, Deep Throat, whose identity has just been made known in *Vanity Fair* as Mark Felt, now 91 years of age. At the time of Watergate he was the number two man in the FBI. Gerald Ford was sworn into the presidency and then, to heal a wounded nation, magnanimously pardoned his predecessor. It was a year burned into the national psyche.

When I left the homestead that year I moved into a furnished apartment on the north side of Rochester. A friend and coworker at the tax office who had been transferred to the Albany office had just vacated the apartment. Jack sometimes stayed overnight and one morning after he did my landlord said to me, "I didn't know you had a friend," referring, I knew, to my overnight visitor. My impudent response was, "Doesn't everybody have a friend?" While living there Evie and Wendy visited me a few times. Two of those times, we telephoned Roy in Iceland around the holidays.

The years between 1972 and 1977 become a blur in my own psyche. As viewed in later years, I realize now that I walked out on family and home in an alcoholic bottom, a common term in AA. I was alone and rudderless. I had no future; I had no goals or dreams. I was on my own after nearly 23 years of marriage. I was the mistress of a married man, and as such met him always and only at his convenience. Still blind to the effect of alcohol on my life, I blamed everything on myself - or God. I had no real faith. When my children were small, I made a fruitless search for a church to raise them in, believing (for some reason I cannot explain) that religious education should be part of their lives. One of the churches held the belief that no one should ever smoke or drink. Since I did both at the time, I decided against that denomination. During drives in the country, which has always been an excellent pastime for me, I thought seriously about ending my life. All I had to do, I told myself, was hit a tree or a bridge abutment. Something always stayed me. My only self-identity was as the parent of four rapidly maturing children, growing out of my life. Because of this flawed memory, I will tell you what I recall about those five years, but they will not necessarily be in chronological order.

I had a wrenching experience in 1974. I went to my ob-gyn doctor for a routine pap smear. Afterward the doctor told me that I was pregnant. I said I couldn't be. What I really meant was that I didn't *want* to be, so how could it happen? The sick mind of an alcoholic has a reasoning all its own; no logic, no sense, and no reason. The doctor sensed my amazement and said that if I did not want to carry it to term I could have a suction abortion, which had become legal because of the US Supreme Court decision in Roe v. Wade in January of 1973. I went to Strong for the procedure, but upon examining me, the ER doctor said you are 20 weeks pregnant. I was incredulous. Suction abortion was illegal at this point in pregnancy. I had had menstrual periods off and on, but chalked it up to the change of life. Nor had I put on a lot of weight. I asked him what I could do, and he told me to go back to the ob-gyn doctor to discuss the now required major surgery.

I left the ER in tears, confused and angry with myself, wishing I were in a terrible nightmare that would end. But I was not. I called a friend and told her I had to talk to someone. I knew in every fiber of my being that I was not emotionally, mentally, physically or financially prepared to give birth to a baby. I was very much alone and struggling to make it on my own. Yet every pregnancy I ever had was an event of joyous anticipation. It was the hardest decision I had ever made. The specialist gave me choices, one of which was to remove the uterus but leave the ovaries for production of estrogen. I chose that option, and have always been glad that I did. Just prior to being wheeled into surgery, the nurse asked if my husband would be there. I said, No he would not. No one was there. My aloneness was profound. I would never be the same, and yet I knew that I would never regret it, either. Later I learned that the embryo could very likely have been a victim of fetal alcohol syndrome because of my excessive drinking

During this period, my drinking continued to escalate. By my drinking escalating, I mean that my consumption increased in quantity and my tolerance increased accordingly. One evening I drank several Black Russians at a bar with Jack. When I got out of the car back home, my legs gave out and I was on my knees by the curb. Jack helped me to my feet and into the apartment, where I went to my knees again, now at the toilet bowl, vomiting. Because of my love affair with alcohol, the only thing that experience taught me was to stay away from Black Russians after that.

I hesitate to make this story a drunkalogue - a series of stories about drunken episodes - but children, the only way to help you understand the disease which you are prone to by genetic transfer is in telling you how the drug's abuse can lead a person to insane thinking, erratic behavior, emotional swings and physical depletion. En route home from drinking heavily with a friend one night, I was stopped by a police officer on a country road. I already had points against my license, and was concerned about getting enough to lose it. I got out of my car and went back to the cop's car (not recommended) and, breathing in his face as he sat in the patrol car, asked, "How many points will this be?" I do not recall whether he gave me a ticket but I recall the audacity I had to ask him this question and to insult his senses with my breath. That was before breathalyzer tests, DWI's, etc. Then I considered myself lucky, but now I know that it would have been in my best interest if I had been charged. Perhaps a court experience would have awakened me to my disease. Perhaps not. When the American Psychiatric Association recognized alcoholism as a disease treatment programs began to emerge. Currently, thank God, there is a spectrum of treatment modalities to help identify and treat the alcohol-dependent person find a sober, useful and rewarding life. The worst incident while driving drunk was the night I hit a tree on the wrong side of the road. It was about 4:00 AM and I was returning home from a friend's house in Newark, New York. As I drove down a desolate country road (which I cannot even name) I realized I was getting sleepy so I opened the window and turned up the radio. Suddenly I awoke to the sight of tree bark in front of me, just an instant before I hit the tree dead on. The headlights remained aglow in my Volkswagen. As I got out of the car, I felt blood streaming down the front of me. I lay down on the ground, thinking I was dying. I said, God I've had a full life; I'm ready to go. I continued to lie there and realized I wasn't dying after all! As I rose and walked to the road, I saw headlights approaching, so I flagged down the car. The driver was a farmer who lived nearby, driving an unlicensed farm truck, so he had to go home to get a licensed car in which to take me to the nearest hospital. While he changed cars, I was invited in to the kitchen, where his wife was cooking breakfast in her spic and span clothing with a lovely frilled apron. I felt like a cruddy tramp in comparison.

When we got to the emergency entrance of the hospital we found it locked! That was a first for me. I thanked the farmer for his trouble just as an attendant opened the door. My stay lasted three days, during which time my daughter Evie came to see me. I asked her to find out where the car was taken and see if my eyeglasses were in it. When she returned, she said she was glad she had seen me before she saw the car. Although the car was totaled and the steering wheel broken in two places, my glasses were on the floor of the front seat, unscathed. The doctor told me that I had not broken my nose but had dislodged the cartilage and he recommended that I have surgery two months hence, which I did. Jack came to discharge me from the hospital, without comment about my accident.

In 1975 I decided to move to the country and found a second floor flat between Avon and Lima, on Works Road. The house has since been razed. Wendy visited me on weekends, and during that period, I received a tax refund, so Wendy and I went on a shopping spree for new clothes. Then one weekend Wendy asked me if she could live with me. I said of course. But I knew finances would be tight. I sought child support. Not far from my new home lived some drinking friends of Jack and mine. (Of course, all of our friends drank.) Once, as we were visiting Bill and Kitty in their home, Bill asked me if I would join his sales team. He was the local representative of a collection agency. His wife said, "Don't do it. You'd be crazy to quit a secure state job for a sales job." In spite of her advice I made a very bad decision and quit the job with the tax department. I felt that I wouldn't know if I could sell unless I tried. My first sales call was a success, but a few weeks later, it became painfully clear that I was not good at selling. I found a bookkeeping job at a photography studio. The pay was sufficient and I always enjoyed working with numbers. Part of my job was to count the cash brought in by the photographer from taking local school pictures, which he left in my desk drawer.

One morning, when there was no cash in my desk, I went to the boss and told him. He said that I was above suspicion, but reported it to the police who came to the studio to investigate. I was asked, as a matter of routine, to take a lie detector test - the kind in which voice vibrations record responses. All employees had to take it. Then everyone had to take it a second time. During my second testing, I made the offhand remark that I would be a good candidate since I had recently gone through bankruptcy. It would end my employment there. Now I became a prime suspect because of that glib remark. The bosses thought bankruptcy was a very immoral act. I had to go to the police department in downtown Rochester (the studio was in the suburbs) for another lie detector test. I said that I would go elsewhere to call my lawyer and they said I could call from there. When I told them that someone had listened in on my phone conversations previously, they naturally denied it. The bottom line was I did not trust them. I knew it was the end of my job, but it was not the end of the criminal investigation. I called my lawyer from a pay phone, in tears. For the first time in my life, a stranger had considered me a thief, and I knew I was not guilty. My lawyer asked if she wanted me to be with her for the lie detector test downtown. Immediately calculating her fee for that, I told her no. She advised me to remain calm, and if at any time, I got uncomfortable during the test to stop and tell them I wouldn't continue without her presence. The test downtown consisted of sensors placed on my arms. It was a time of great distress; I was a target of suspicion and now jobless. Of course, the test showed that I was innocent and so I was not charged. A few weeks after I left the studio I ran into one of the photographers, who told me that they had caught an employee with all the keys to the office in his pocket, but I shouldn't expect an apology. His prediction was proven accurate a few weeks later. As I was crossing an intersection in downtown Rochester - at the corner of Exchange & Broad Street - one of the owners of the photo studio was crossing from the opposite direction and as we neared each other, he said, "Do you have the bag with you?", implying I still had the company funds. He did not apologize, did not acknowledge the real culprit had been found, nor offered me the job back again. It was clear that he did not know I had learned the truth.

My reason for being downtown that day was that I had taken a full time job as tax consultant at the Four Corners office of E. F. Hutton. They hired me as a tax specialist to file various returns related to customers' tax shelter accounts. I was told the job would eventually be a forty-hour workweek, but at the time, there were only about 20 hours of work per week. It was a small office, not one with public access, so I spent some time reading to while away the time. Interestingly enough, my coworker told me she went to West High at the same time I did. I didn't remember her; maybe that was why she became so unfriendly. On the other hand, maybe it was because I found an unfiled tax return from the previous year in the file cabinet one day (which I proceeded to file late). She told me I could not read on the job. I started taking time off when there was no work to do. One day she came to me and told me that I should quit. One of the unwritten rules of employment is that you go to your immediate boss with a problem, but I knew that in this case it was necessary for me to go over her head. The boss at the next level was a man with whom I could communicate. Maybe because his last name was Wallace! So the first chance I got I told him that I had a daughter to support and would he please fire me so I could apply for unemployment. Work was not easy to find, as the economy was in a recession in 1975. Additionally, I could not get a good reference now from the photo studio. I finally took a job at a Neisner's warehouse, putting price tags on clothing. I was punching the time clock four times a day: In, out, and lunchtime in and out. The work included hauling large bundles of clothes, which were too heavy for me to handle. I lasted three weeks and then quit. How was I going to support Wendy and myself now, I asked myself. I applied for social services assistance for the first time in my life. I didn't like the idea, but felt I had no choice. Applying for unemployment was not an option since I had quit the job at Neisner's. However, when I went to social services, they told me to apply for unemployment because the job was not consistent with my work history. My background was office work, accounting, bookkeeping. I applied for and received unemployment insurance. My lawyer obtained child support which made it easier to provide Wendy with a home.

Through those years I drove various Volkswagens. I had a lot of fun in those little cars. They were dependable, easy to park and only became a problem in the wintertime when the air-cooled engine failed to provide sufficient heat. One day while I was driving with Wendy on West Henrietta Road, the engine caught fire. I quickly pulled into a parking lot in front of a store, calling to Wendy to get out. The store owner rushed out with a fire extinguisher and put the fire out. The car had to be towed to the garage. Not realizing that I could have had the wiring replaced, I assumed I needed another car. Jack helped me find another vehicle to drive - yes, another Volkswagen.

When we built the cottage, I purchased an apartment sized stove that was for sale on the roadside as we went to the cottage one day. The car's passenger seat was removable, so I took it out and tossed it in the back seat, placing the stove where the seat had been. Evie rode in the back seat the rest of the way to the cottage. In addition, when a friend and her husband bought a piece of property in the country to build on, we drove all over the field in my Volkswagen. Almost fell in a chuckhole! The best Volkswagen story is the day that the same neighbor with her five kids joined my four kids and me in a Volkswagen and drove to Mendon Ponds Park for a swim. It was a very hot day and worth the crammed trip. As we got out of the car, a group of nuns who were having a picnic came over and said, "Did all of you really get out of that car?" In 1974, while living on Works Road, I bought a brand new yellow Volkswagen; it was my first new one. But finances became very tight and I lost the car in bankruptcy proceedings.

One winter evening Evie came to visit Wendy and me. Soon after she left, I received a phone call from Marty, who now lived a few miles away. He told me Evie had been in a car accident and was in the emergency room at Strong. I said, "She was just here!" I immediately went to her. She had spun out on the icy road nearby, hitting a mailbox and smashing her window. The slivers of glass in her arms took weeks to surface, but with the best of fortune, she was not critically hurt.

When Wendy completed high school, she decided to attend Monroe Community College. Knowing transportation would be a problem, I realized we would have to move closer to the campus. Thus it was that we took an apartment across the street from MCC and Wendy began classes. Two months after the term began she met Ed, another student. He was a veteran, one of many attending classes at the time. She fell in love with him and announced that they would be married. He was six years her senior, at 23. It wasn't long before she told me that they had set the date for the wedding. I was furious. She was a good student and I hoped she would get the education I did not. Before the wedding I yelled at her, in his presence, "Marry him and you'll regret it!" I did not find any fault in Ed; it was just that I was so angry with him for diverting her mind from education to marriage.

They did get married, with Rev. Cayley officiating, the same minister who had married Steve and me 27 years earlier. It was June 1976. My anger gradually dissolved into pride, as I saw them taking their vows. Evie offered to hold a barbecue reception at her country home, where they raised buffaloes. I agreed to parboil 20 chickens but as I did so, I regretted that offer. Cooking one chicken is fine, but the aroma that emanates from boiling multiple chickens is, to say the least, obnoxious. To honor the bride and groom on that lovely summer day, a fine crowd gathered at the buffalo ranch where Evie lived with her husband. My baby, my youngest, was married.

The United States celebrated its bicentennial in 1976, and it seemed to be the year of new freedom for the Douglas children. Marty also married that year. Steve and I were, of course, invited to the wedding and reception, where we were assigned different tables. Probably it was my guilt over leaving him that made me feel like an outcast. Ed, Wendy's new husband, asked me to dance, and that eased the pain of the moment. Evie had married, very quietly, in 1975. Roy enrolled at New York State University in Plattsburgh. They all had their own lives which kept them very busy, and I didn't see much of them. I was lonelier than ever, though Jack and I continued to spend every weekend together and vacationed together. As a winner in a sales promotion, he won the top prize: a weekend at Greenbrier, in West Virginia. It was a splendid retreat where large corporations send their executives for rest and relaxation. Its luxury stood in stark contrast to the impoverished people in the surrounding area.

The vacation prize Jack received was supposed to be for the winner and his spouse. However, under the circumstances Jack asked me to stand in as his wife. I had no problem with the deception. We would be with people I had never met and would never see again. We flew to Washington, DC and took a small plane to an airport nearby, then a cab to Greenbrier. It was a luxurious weekend. A little too luxurious, I think, when Jack was denied admittance to the dining room until he donned a jacket for breakfast. There were two golf courses, carriage rides around the grounds, a movie theater and bowling alleys. We decided to take in a movie titled, curiously enough, "Weekend Affair." Another salesperson there that Jack knew joined us for dinner, with his wife. During the course of the conversation, his wife asked how many children we had. Simultaneously Jack said six and I said four. It was embarrassing, but the conversation slid right over it and we enjoyed the evening. Jack was always generous and treated me very well. Our relationship lasted seven years, but in all that time there never was a picture taken of us together. We both carried guilt over the situation, but not enough guilt to end it. As good as Jack was to me, at some point I realized that he would never leave his wife for me, so I would have to settle, indefinitely, for being a mistress instead of a wife.

During the seventh year of our relationship, I read about three Walden Two communities. They were groups established on the democratic principles set forth in Thoreau's writings about Walden Pond. I wrote to them asking for more information. One community was in North Carolina, one was in Missouri, and the other was in Virginia. The first two responded, advising that I could visit under a work-exchange program, without cost, by agreeing to perform various tasks at the community in exchange for room and board. I signed up for a visit to Missouri. I was still on unemployment and had to report every two weeks, so I could spend only 10 days there; four days were required for traveling. I packed all my belongings and departed, homeless now. I needed the money for traveling, so I didn't have enough for rent, too. The night before leaving, I stayed over at the cottage. Before I left I noticed the floor under the battery (behind the driver's seat) was eroding away. After a friend secured it he told me to "hang onto it" while I traveled. It lasted the trip.

I left for Missouri, taking with me the complete lunch that my friend Marion packed for me - including dessert. I bought a bottle of cheap wine. I found a cheap motel to stay in overnight at the halfway point. I don't recall where. As I passed through St. Louis, I saw the St. Louis Arch, a relatively new structure then. Upon arrival at the community, the first building I saw was the imposing main building. In it were a huge common room, a large kitchen and a dining area. When I arrived, there were several people there talking, reading, listening to music. As I read the literature about the place, I quickly realized that the outdoor toilets and showers were co-ed! A woman in her fifties came over to me and said, I will tell you about an outhouse that most of the people here don't use. It's a little farther away, but it will afford you some privacy. I was very appreciative. Regarding the co-ed showers, one day as I entered the shower room I realized, as I opened the door that there was a young couple showering. I quickly pulled back, apologizing. They said, "Come on in, you are welcome." However, I declined the invitation.

On the floor of this huge main building, there were several crates of potatoes, apples and other produce. Everything was bought in bulk because approximately sixty people lived there. Besides the main building, there were three dormitory buildings, with another under construction. Additionally, there were buildings for production of the items sold by the community - hammocks and sandals. The community exemplified a democracy in action; everyone had a job to do and equality prevailed. The tasks in the main house were posted and everyone had to sign up for a two hour stint. One day I signed up for washing pots and pans after supper. When I went to the kitchen for my task, I could hardly believe my eyes. I had seen the huge kettles and pots used in restaurants, but the number of them piled up and dirty staggered my imagination. It took me three hours to clean them all. It was such a long task that people playing cards in the dining room noticed, and when I finished they all applauded me! The next day I learned that the person scheduled to wash the pots and pans after lunch had failed to do the job. Later, the identified person came to me and apologized.

My production job was in the large warehouse, building hammocks. There were other buildings for weaving, woodworking, and shellacking. About 20 to 30 of us worked on the hammocks. There was a radio and it presented an example of the democratic methods used. Everyone could choose the kind of music that we heard, for a period of 30 minutes. One person opted for his 30 minutes to have the radio turned off! There were paths between the buildings, and small lights along the paths showed the way. The residents were free to choose whatever sexual relationship they desired, so there were various sexual relationships, but everyone was discreet in their sexual behavior. Respect of all residents was paramount. Some residents were single and happily so. They just wanted to be there, away from society and its demands. Except for the administrators, I was the only one with a car. Part of the agreement to live there was that you give up all your worldly possessions. One day the administrators asked me if I would make a trip to the nearby town for a few supplies. I agreed and while there, I bought a bottle of wine to have on my last night.

The community's arrangement reminded me of socialism: "From each according to his ability, to each according to his need." (It was a definition Joy had given me years before.) When I left there, I learned that a medical doctor would soon be coming to care for the needs of the residents. All the Walden communities kept in touch with each other. Two or three older people asked me to consider staying at the commune to live. I did consider it for a time. However, giving up my car was not an easy option. When I had been unable to pay rent at the apartment near MCC, I realized that I had to make a choice: run out on the lease or give up my car. Then, and now, my car represents a freedom which I am unwilling to forfeit. Cozily seated in front of a fireplace with a roaring fire, I spent my last evening sharing my bottle of wine with some of the residents. They wished me well. I left

Missouri with a passenger who had posted her wishes on a bulletin board to join anyone traveling near Erie, Pennsylvania. Her companionship made the trip more enjoyable.

When I returned I called Jack and he came to the motel I had chosen and spent the weekend with me. Two weeks later, I left for the North Carolina Walden community. It was much smaller than the one in Missouri. The only product made there was a line of designer tin cans. A very talented young man took ordinary tin cans, applied a blowtorch and burned holes in scroll-like patterns. I still have one of the smaller #2 cans for holding pens and pencils. Larger coffee cans held flowerpots, etc. This place was more rural, with a cow, a pig, and some chickens. Only about 20 people lived in this rustic setting and I had to sleep in my sleeping bag in the barn loft with others, but I had my privacy. This new community was in the process of installing a drainage system. I took my turns at that task. It was a new experience to leave a job, and see the progress made overnight. It was true community sharing of work. During my visit, a young female resident of the commune took me with her to sell the tin can art ware in nearby Winston-Salem. We packed all the cans carefully and set up our stand at a local fair. To my surprise, we sold over $200. worth, probably because it was early December and people were shopping for Christmas. After the sale, we attended a chamber music concert; something I had never done before. Just before I left, I went out into the woods to see if I could find a tiny fir tree to take home for my Christmas. I dug it up and packed it in the car. I took several of the tin cans with me, to sell for the community, but I guess their trust was misplaced. I never did sell any or send them any money. Another good example of poor behavior, another example of the stinking thinking of an alcoholic. I had no money for family Christmas gifts so I decided to use the cans as Christmas presents for my children.

After the holidays, as 1977 dawned, I was living in a single room off East Ave, drinking daily, reporting to the unemployment office biweekly. I kept a bottle of vodka in the dresser drawer to protect the supply, an alcoholic behavior. I am not sure how I spent my weekdays, but I spent my weekends with Jack. Somehow, the car kept running efficiently so I didn't have repair expenses. Then I remembered a community in the Adirondacks - for women only. It was called A Woman's Place, but it is no longer there. I contacted them and signed up for ten days of work-exchange. Once more, I asked my friend Marion to pack a lunch for my trip as she had done for the previous two trips. On that cold February day as she put a fine lunch in a box, I said to her, "Marion, there is something about the trip that is different from the others. I don't know why, but I feel that it is going to be different." Little did I know that the trip was going to change the entire course of my life. I want to explain why I wanted to visit a community of all women. Ever since I was young, about eleven years old, I occasionally met another female toward whom I felt a strong attraction, not even identifying it with a sexual attraction, merely a desire to be near her and spend time with her. Of course not all females affected me that way, but every once in a while I met someone who seemed very attractive to me. I could not explain the feelings, nor did I understand them, but they were there all the same. I never overtly expressed these feelings. I had heard about the book *The Well of Loneliness* and wanted to read it because of the controversy it caused, but I was afraid to ask for it in any library or store, lest I have that forbidden identity. In going to A Woman's Place maybe I could find out for myself what these feelings meant, if anything. At least I would have the opportunity to explore them.

I bought a bottle of wine en route. On the way, I said to myself, What if I find out that my attraction to women is my real identity? In addition, what are the

100

chances of meeting someone in such a short visit? Was I crazy - going to a strange place to spend a week or more with many people I had never met before? Nevertheless, I was on the way; the die was cast. By the time I started up the Northway (Route I-89) from Albany to Montreal, it began to snow, and it became worse by the minute, all the rest of the way. Warrensburg, a little town just north of Lake George, was the last settlement I went through. Then I had to continue another four or five miles up the mountain to the retreat. The last few miles were ominous; the snow-covered road made driving difficult, visibility poor. Finally I arrived at my destination and was greeted at the door by a woman who said she wasn't expecting me that night. I said that I could turn around and head back to Rochester but would rather not. She said, "Oh no, come in and enjoy the fire." It was a welcome sight, and a warm one. She offered me a cup of coffee. She was the only one there at the time, but others would be coming in to spend the weekend.

Dozens of women converged on the retreat, from Friday evening to Saturday afternoon. Many came from New York City. Some were single, others came in couples. All had been there before, so it was much like a reunion. Besides the main building, with a huge community room and a large kitchen, the retreat also had five or six cabins. Across the road was a pond for swimming. Saturday evening one woman came in from the local area. Her name was Pam. We chatted about the retreat, the weather, etc. and I walked her to her car. As we brushed the snow off her car, I made an offhand comment about "first things first." Her eyes lit up, as though I had spoken some password. She returned the next day and in the course of our conversation, she explained that first things first was one of the slogans of Alcoholics Anonymous, of which she was a member. I thought how unfortunate she could not drink, because drinking was such a significant part of my life. Every day, after I completed

101

my chores I met her in town for coffee. We became friends, and I told her that since I had a tax refund coming perhaps I could return with it and we could see some movies and eat out. She agreed it would be a good idea.

Chapter 4: My Life Takes a New Direction

1977-1987; Age 48-58

As I drove back to Rochester, I had something to look forward to - returning to the retreat and spending time with a new friend. I took a room in a motel and signed up for unemployment. Daily drinking and my affair with Jack continued. When the tax refund came, I quickly made plans to return. I told Jack that I would be back in two weeks. Little did I know that it was in fact the end of our relationship. Nor did I have the slightest notion that I would not return in two weeks. I never did see him again to explain anything. This was yet another example of my inability or unwillingness to communicate my feelings or my situation to someone else. I knew that he still had his wife and their home together. I packed all my books and all my clothes (a very small wardrobe, indeed) into my car. I learned later that as I pulled up with my Volkswagen full of clothes and books, Pam was worried that I had a permanent idea in mind. We proceeded to spend my cache of cash, enjoying the current flicks and eating at the Ponderosa. It was not love at first sight, but as we conversed and shared our experiences with each other, we grew fonder of each other, which led to a sexual relationship. It proved to me that all the urges I had had through my earlier years were real, and I found great pleasure in my first homosexual relationship, although we had separate living quarters. Pam had a room in the house where three other boarders lived and I had one of the motel rooms next door. We planned our days around each other's activities.

I was inordinately happy. In spite of the fact that I was still collecting unemployment insurance, I had someone to share life with; someone who was intelligent, had a sense of humor and an interest in a variety of things. During this time, the proprietor and his wife decided to close the motel and turn it into an antique shop, which until then was in their large garage. Perhaps foreseeing my continued stay, they remodeled the garage into a one-bedroom apartment, complete with kitchen. The rent was very low and I gladly moved in. Now I could cook for the two of us, but Pam remained in the house lest she lose her social services income. Her intent was to find work in the North Country, but ill health coupled with unemployment forced her to apply for welfare. Together we wrote a grocery list, and I planned and cooked the meals. I made a biweekly trip to Rochester to sign for unemployment until one sign-in day I found out that I had to move back to the area or transfer my unemployment checks to my new residence. Therefore, I transferred them. I was not making any long-range plans; I liked the way my life was at the time. Our social life became AA, as we attended meetings all over the North Country. I never spoke at meetings except to give my name and say that I was a visitor. We both had cars, but I drove most of the time because I got better mileage on my vehicle.

When I received my last unemployment check, I knew I had to get a job; there was not much opportunity in the Lake George area, so I traveled to Albany in search of work. I bought a copy of the *Albany Times-Union* and scanned the want ads. It was lunchtime so I knew it was not a good time to seek work. At the lunch hour I decided to go to the top of the Corning Tower. I stood on the observation deck atop the building and asked myself, what now? With no resources in sight, I silently asked God for guidance, but I have no idea why, except to say that when we hit a seemingly insurmountable wall and have no options, God alone seems to be our resource. On the other hand, perhaps because of all the AA meetings where I constantly heard about a Higher Power, I decided to call on Him. My silent thought was where is my life going now? Should I turn tail and return to Rochester? Nothing awaited me - no home and a dead-end relationship with a married man who would never leave his wife for me. My children were all married and settled down. I certainly could not see myself living with any of them, and at that time, they did not have the space anyhow.

The ads listed a job on Park Avenue for a part time bookkeeper, but no ads for full time work. So I looked for the address - and looked some more. Park Avenue seemed to end before I found the number I sought. After inquiring, I learned that the Empire State Plaza interrupts Park Avenue, which extends on either side of it. I finally located the place in the afternoon and was hired on the spot by the owner. Pam was incredulous when I told her I had a job already. It would not be easy to survive on part time work, but I would have to try. I took a room in Albany on Hudson Avenue, sharing the bath. I did have a sink in my room, which was a blessing the day I went to the bathroom to find a sign on the door "Do not open door; bat inside!" This was a completely new experience for me, but someone told me later that there are many bats in Albany. I never saw one, however, after that experience. Pam came weekends and sometimes I went up to see her during the week. My boss invited me and a friend to his daughter's wedding, so Pam and I went. It was a huge, elaborate reception in a local banquet hall. It was the first and only time I ever saw each place setting with not only an extensive number of pieces of silverware, but also six glasses!

Longing for a room with a bath of my own, I moved into one on Lake Avenue, near the Capital District Psychiatric Center (CDPC). Wendy and her husband came to visit me there, but I wasn't home and they didn't know where to find me so they returned to Rochester. When I read their note, I was very disappointed that I had missed them. They had come to see me knowing I could not attend a pending baby shower for Wendy. Travel was out of the question at the time; it was all I could do to survive financially. I couldn't even send a shower gift.

For diversion, one weekend Pam and I attended a weekend Women's Conference at Adirondack Community College. In accord with my habit of reading everything in print that I encounter, I read the college's bulletin board for students. There was an advertisement for an experienced bookkeeper. I wondered how many kids attending college would qualify for this job. I applied, and a company that manufactures stage scenery and scrims (stage backdrop curtains) hired me. Back to the North Country I went, happy to have a job in the mountains. I especially remember the scrim they made for an Eagles concert in Calgary, and the Olympic logo of rings for the 1980 Olympic Games at Lake Placid, New York. With a regular income, Pam and I could have a more comfortable life. Pam had been unable to find work and then ill health intervened so that she had to apply for disability insurance.

 The first two years with Pam were comfortable and relatively peaceful. Pam and I liked to read, have intelligent conversations, were curious about many things in life, and we both had a sense of humor. She had an avid interest in Saratoga Springs and in the Olympics, held in Lake Placid in 1980 - the year that Wayne Gretsky and the young US Hockey team beat the favored Russian team. Her interest in Saratoga Springs and horseracing led me to an interest in the Kentucky Derby and other national races. I don't recall, though, that we ever went to the racetrack in Saratoga. In fact, in August (racing season there) we deliberately went around it on the Northway, because of the traffic congestion. Yet it was a limited kind of relationship; our social life consisted of attending AA meetings. We went to meetings all around the area and sometimes, on weekends, we attended meetings in Albany, 60 miles south of us. We made few friends but had many acquaintances in AA. We did not experience any homophobia, but sometimes others seemed to sense our relationship and distanced themselves. Because of the low population in the mountains and the population's tendency toward homophobia, there were no gay meetings in the North Country.

We took in a movie now and then and ate out frequently. As time went on, I realized that my partner had a problem with control - over my activities and me. However, since no one had ever taken that much interest in me, I enjoyed it immensely. Progressively she reached into my life. Although she meant well, the smothering became a little too much when she called my auto mechanic to advise him not to charge me too much because I didn't make a lot of money; or another time when she called my employer, telling him I was having "family problems" and he should be considerate of me! I was 200 miles from my family, and did hear about their personal tribulations, but the children seemed very capable of resolving their issues and I never felt it was necessary to return to Rochester because of them. I raised them and now they were on their own. Sometimes Wendy or Evie would mention the possibility of my moving back, but something seemed to keep me there. I have no idea why at that time I wasn't drawn back to be with my grandchildren. I made the trip to Rochester every time a new grandchild was born, but something kept me in eastern New York State. In retrospect, I can see that my life simply was not making me a "baby-sitting grandma," as it took one turn after another, for a relationship, for an education, and finally, as a spiritual seeker. The first grandchild came on October 8, 1978. After a long and arduous labor, Evie, my first-born, gave birth to Owen, her first-born.

Shortly after I returned to work a coworker, Linda, told me about a local psychic reader. Linda said that she had become a "believer" in spirit communication after Millie, in Lake George, had told her things about Linda that no one could ever know about. Linda said to me, "You have to go and see her!" I had never been to a psychic in my life, nor did I know anything about them. I made an appointment merely out of curiosity. Since Millie permitted tape recording of her readings, I took a recorder with me. She would hold the microphone herself and turn it off when she began telling personal stories of her own psychic experiences. On my first visit, she immediately saw my father standing behind me, describing him as tall and good-looking. His first message to me was that he just could not catch his breath. He was speaking of himself just before dying! I recalled that he had lain down for a morning nap and never rose from it. Millie said he was sitting on a large rock, noting, "I don't know what that means." I agreed that it made no sense to me either. She asked me if I had had female surgery because she "saw" the scar, though I was fully dressed. I told her yes I had had a hysterectomy. She correctly noted that I was having problems with my back, and suggested I change the kind of chair I sat on at work. To my complaint that I was having dreams about water, she answered that the noise in the factory, which shared a common wall with the office area, was so disturbing that dreams of water were a calming influence on me. After an hour, as she came to the end of my allotted time, she said she saw me outside a one-room schoolhouse, yanking on a bell outside the door, summoning the children to class. She described my physical appearance - similar to me at this time - short, brown hair, pulled back in a bun, wearing wire-rimmed glasses. I told her I had never been a teacher and she said what she was seeing was me in a past life, in Missouri at the time of US westward expansion.

On the way home that night I mulled over what I had heard. What could Dad sitting on the rock mean? Suddenly I recalled that childhood experience when I cut my knee and Dad carried me into the office to treat it. Yes, a rock was the only worldly thing that made a connection between my father and me. He must surely have come to me to identify him and assure me that he was still very much alive. He had said, through Millie, that he was waiting for me and wanted to show me around there because there the colors are different, the light is different. I became a believer myself in the concept that those who have gone before us - the "dead" are really still very much alive, can, and do communicate with us earthlings. I called Millie for a second reading. Her comment about a past life of mine piqued my curiosity and I wanted to hear more. She said she could not guarantee more past life information, but would see what she could get for me. On my second visit to her, the first thing she told me was the same description of me in Missouri as a schoolteacher! She then proceeded to describe four other lifetimes that I had lived! She described me as a two-year-old girl, arriving in Boston Harbor in the 17th century with my parents. My father was a minister. She jumped ahead to my teen years and saw me writing down my father's sermons as he paced near my desk and spoke them aloud so I could write them down for him to read the next Sunday. I think I admired him greatly and desired to emulate him, but women were not allowed in the ministry then. Even now, some churches forbid it. Then Millie saw me as a young girl living with an aunt and my grandmother near Paris, France, in about the 18th century. My wealthy father came to take me to live with him and his mother in Paris and raise me. We drove off in a buggy after a tearful farewell and in Paris I met and married a man who was later killed by a runaway horse on the street. I returned to find my aunt living alone; grandmother had died. I asked my aunt to return to Paris and live with me. She accepted.

Next Millie saw me as the wife of an Irish innkeeper in the 15th century. She saw me on my hands and knees, scrubbing the floor of the barroom and cursing under my breath about the cleaning the floors where the men spat. Apparently, cuspidors had not yet been invented. We had two young children, a boy and a girl. Possibly six and eight years old. One day I was in bed, in agony. The children saw me from the doorway, wondering. My husband came in and said, "Are you that way again?" I said no. Millie said a doctor came but she commented, "He doesn't know anything about medicine." Millie said I died soon after of a ruptured appendix.

The last lifetime Mille described was in Greece or Rome. I was married to "someone who makes laws"; I presume a senator. Interestingly enough, the further back Millie went in time the more details she provided. In this last lifetime, she described me as a teenager living in a wealthy family. I told my parents I wanted to travel the world, but they said I needed an escort to do that. I responded that I *had* an escort. Way back then, I was pretty strong-willed. She then saw me married to the senator and helping him in his work. Then she described the scene of his death. My husband was descending the steps of a large building as a chariot raced down the street toward him. The passenger got off the chariot, ran up the steps and killed my husband. Millie saw me sitting by a window deeply grieving.

Twice after that, I consulted Millie again, once taking pictures of my children for her to read for me. I taped all of the readings and occasionally play them again, but recall vividly some of the comments. It would be four more years before I would encounter another psychic, but it is still comforting indeed to know that my father will be there to welcome me when I go home to that place of Light and Love.

After three years in Warrensburg I became restless to do something more with my life. The job was fine, but it had no future. I liked the work, but there were frequent disagreements among my three bosses. In addition, the noise of the production room - hammering, sawing, drilling etc. was cacophony to my ears. Furthermore, Pam's continuing efforts at controlling my life became stifling. My drinking slowed down considerably during the time I lived in the North Country, but I usually did have a bottle in my room, which Pam found one day and berated me for it, telling me she thought I was an alcoholic like herself. In my mind, I thought she was merely projecting her problems onto me, so I ignored her comment. I had attended AA meetings for three years, always stating that my name is Ellen and I am a visitor. It was a perfect example of denial, denial, denial. Members in the meetings probably were aware of this attitude of denial, which is so prevalent in problem drinkers. I still was clueless about the disaster alcohol had made of my life, but I knew that my mother, two brothers and at least one sister were alcoholics, so I decided to help others with that problem and I set my sights on becoming an alcoholism counselor.

I gathered information from SUNY Albany, Empire State College and Russell Sage College to obtain a bachelors degree in counseling. In the course of learning about graduate degrees, I learned to my amazement that a graduate degree need not be in the same discipline as one's bachelor's degree. After considering all my options, I chose Russell Sage College and enrolled in the master's degree in Community Psychology. Of the three tracks offered, I chose Alcohol and Drug Counseling. I was under the impression that to become a counselor I needed a degree in counseling. Later I learned that an academic degree was not essential. I could have merely taken the six required courses in the counseling track. I began classes in the summer session, in 1980, without the benefit of an advisor. It was a mistake because the accelerated summer sessions were condensed and I was not prepared. Nine years had passed since I had sat in a classroom. Nevertheless, I received a passing grade and signed up for three subjects in the fall evening session. It was a very busy spring in 1980. I began classes at RSC, found an apartment on Elm Street, and started a job as Fiscal Officer at a local counseling agency. Everything just fell into place for me - except I did not communicate my intentions to Pam. In my mind, I believed the relationship to be over, so that was it. Never having learned good communication skills, I was under the impression that she would read my mind and know that we were through. She did not read it at all, and tried to get me back into the relationship. She would occasionally come to Albany for a visit and one evening we argued so loudly that Pam worried my landlady would hear. I said the landlady knew what was going on. At the peak of my raging, I stormed out of the apartment and drove around downtown Albany. All of a sudden, I thought what am I doing. I should be in my own place and Pam should do the leaving! My habit of running away from a problem instead of facing it was ludicrously apparent to me that night. I returned to the apartment and told Pam to leave. This tumultuous relationship continued throughout my first year at Sage before I ended it for good. One evening in particular I was walking to the Sage campus (Junior College of Albany shared its campus with Russell Sage College in Troy, NY) crying as I went, upset about the rocky relationship. I knew I couldn't calm down for the class so I returned to my apartment. After I moved to Schenectady, I was advised by a friend to return all the things Pam had left in my apartment, tell her it was all over, and bless her as I left. When I did so, she carried on fiercely, grabbed my arm and pleaded for me not to leave her. Nevertheless, I did, saying as I went God bless you.

While I was living on Elm Street, Marty, who was divorced and had no children, drove his motorcycle to

Albany for a visit. We went to Pittsfield, MA for supper and had a wonderful visit. Wendy also came, with her boyfriend, for a visit. I truly enjoyed it when my children came to visit me. It was a long enough trip, requiring some pre-planning for anyone working a full time job. Driving time is approximately four hours. I never felt that I had to entertain them, and in fact, I could not have afforded to. We just had great talks about our lives and our activities.

I am very grateful for the fact that my children did not press me to return to Rochester. When I finally did, though, they came to pack the van and move me home. What a great gesture and show of support. They were delighted that I was going home again.

Roy visited me on Elm Street, too, on his way to Boston. I'm not sure what made him want to go there, but he stayed with me a day or so and then accepted a ride part way to the coast. I dropped him off on a country road somewhere in Vermont when he said, "This is okay, Mom." As I watched him walk down the road, I had no idea when I would see him again. It turned out to be three years - three years of not knowing just where he was or how he was. I consulted two psychics regarding his whereabouts. One told me that she saw him in Florida; another said that he was in California. The truth was that he never left South Boston. This illustrated for me the truth about psychics. Just as with any other profession, there is a variety of ability. There are excellent mediums and there are wannabe mediums.

The three years I lived on Elm Street I enjoyed watching the July 4 fireworks display at the Empire State Plaza; I could see not only the fireworks but also their reflection in the windows of the 40-story Corning Tower. In the summer of 1983, after not hearing from Roy for three years, he called me at work and said he could see the Albany skyline! I was elated, picked him up at a bar on Central Avenue and offered him my

113

spare bedroom. He spent three days with me. For some reason I had two cars at that time, so I told him he could use my Volkswagen while he was there. He went to Saratoga Springs to visit a friend and his last evening we sat on the back porch and shared a bottle of wine.

On the national scene in 1981, President Reagan appointed Sandra Day O'Connor as the first female judge to the bench of the US Supreme Court. It was a huge breakthrough for women. What with working and attending classes, I had little time for anything else, but I did watch the news on TV, even if I did not have time to read the paper. Somehow, my life has always been full of activities. Whenever I had applied for a job, I laughed at the question what are your hobbies. Hobbies? When I was raising a family, working days and attending classes back at RIT, how in the world could I have had time for hobbies? I would put in photography, which seemed safe enough.

As I took the subjects related to alcoholism, I became very unsettled. Looking back, the information I was learning was beginning to point to my own problems with alcohol. Although I could not explain the pinch I was feeling, it was there. I changed the direction of my studies, abandoned the counseling track and decided it was not for me. In 1983, I noticed an advertisement posted at the counseling center. A treatment center for recovering alcoholic women was seeking a counselor. I wondered if I could fulfill my dream to be a counselor. I applied for the job, had two interviews and got the position as a night respite counselor. Because I was not a NYS credentialed counselor and I was still taking classes at RSC, I took the job with its condition that there was a 90-day probation period. Before leaving, the staff at the counseling center had a farewell party for me at a local bar. In my three years there, I had become very close to my coworkers; we were like a family. Their feeling of attachment to me was demonstrated by an album of pictures (which I still have) they put together to present to me that night. Taking advantage of the open bar, I drank myself into a drunken oblivion and drove home. The next day someone at work said she had followed me home to make sure I got there okay. It struck me as a little strange; what good would an escort do if I were in an accident? Years later, I ran into one of those coworkers who had found out about my alcoholism. She apologized for the farewell party, but I said, "Hey, we had a great time; who knew I had a problem then?"

The first month I worked at The Next Step, a halfway house for female alcoholics, I attended a conference on alcoholism in Niagara Falls. The evening of the first day of the conference, I went to dinner at the restaurant at the top of the building known as the Needle and proceeded to have a few drinks. I returned with alcohol on my breath, of course, but slept all right and got up in the morning on time to attend the second day. A few weeks later, when my probation ended, I lost the job. The administrator told me that I had hidden from the clients with whom I was supposed to interact and observe their behavior as a tool of treatment. Instead, I had spent most of my time in my office, reading. In my own defense, I reminded them that they had assigned a lot of reading. However, the truth of the matter was that I did not know how to interact with the clients and used the reading as an excuse not to.

The staff, at my terminating conference, told me they suspected I might have an alcohol problem and suggested that a group counseling experience as a client would help me understand the dynamics of group therapy as a counselor. Therefore, after leaving the job I found a counselor. I could not afford the fee, so I negotiated a bartering system. The counselor needed work done on her financial records, so I would help her with that in exchange for counseling. We agreed on an hourly rate both ways and we agreed that I would keep track of the hours I spent on her books and the hours I spent in counseling. For a year, we continued in this barter plan; then for another year, I remained in counseling as a paying client after I found work at Planned Parenthood in Schenectady. Under her counseling expertise, first one-on-one and then in group therapy, I dealt with many issues from my early childhood. I pounded pillows and yelled at my mother. I cried and struggled with expressing my feelings - *all* my feelings - something unheard of in my first home. Without realizing it at the time I was dealing with my issues as an adult child of an alcoholic (ACOA). I had anger, hurt and fears that had never been expressed and were just waiting for an outlet in a safe setting.

It was 1983 while working at Planned Parenthood in Schenectady that I began attending Trinity Temple of the Holy Spirit in Albany, at the suggestion of a friend. The Sunday evening service, after the sermon, consisted of three or four psychics standing on the podium and giving messages to various members of the congregation. Except for the messages that I received through Millie in Lake George when I worked in the North Country, it was the first time I heard a psychic give messages. My world at that time did not include the large number of mediums and psychics that I later encountered. The profession is still underground to mainstream society. I am grateful that John Edwards, the Pet Psychic and other TV shows are now available to the public.

Several mediums took turns on the podium at Trinity and the message portion of the service lasted about 20 minutes. Sometimes I received a message. Receiving and hearing others receive messages opened me to a completely new experience. The validity of the messages, confirmed by the responses of the receivers, including myself, proved to me beyond a doubt that life indeed continues after death and communication between residents of the earth and the spirit realm is not only possible but easily attained when one is open to it. I learned early on that no one - no one - can call on a spirit from the other side unless the spirit desires to come (entities in the spirit realm have free will also).

During my first year attending Trinity, one of the members of the Board of Trustees approached me and asked if I would be willing to be a guest speaker some Sunday evening while the Founding Pastor, Rev. Penny Donovan, was on sabbatical leave. I was surprised at the request, but agreed. I had spoken many times at work to groups, so I could probably do so from a church podium. At first, I was nervous because speaking in a holy setting was far more significant to me than lecturing alcoholic clients in a cafeteria. I cannot recall what my topic was but I was relieved to hear that the Board was pleased with its content.

About this time my Elm Street landlady told me that she wanted to move into my apartment and rent out hers, particularly because she had decorated it very nicely. She gave me a few weeks to find something else and move out. I was angry at the request and thought I will move as quickly as I can if that's how it is. My deep and sudden anger surprised me. Sometimes I worked at Planned Parenthood on Saturday to catch up on the record keeping. Sitting at my desk one Saturday morning, alone in the building I said to myself I was going home. Without warning or comprehension, I burst into tears. I did not know why I was crying, I only knew that I was in pain and the pain spilled out in the form of tears. It was not until a year later, in therapy, that I came to understand the pain and its source: As a youngster, I had to move many times without my consent or permission. Marrying and leaving my husband were my personal choices, as were all my ensuing changes of residence. Now, for the first time in nearly thirty years someone told me to move against my wishes. All the old anger, previously stuffed at having to move repeatedly, surfaced.

I found an apartment in the Stockade section of Schenectady, which was within walking distance of my job at Planned Parenthood. It was a small, dark, first-floor apartment in the rear and I had to share the bath with the couple who lived in the front apartment. Evie came with Owen for a visit, but when Owen heard the footsteps of the tenant upstairs, he became frightened and cried. In his young life, he had never lived in a house in which you could hear people walking around upstairs. It was also then that I finally ended my relationship with Pam. Occasionally she would call and we would try again to make a go of our relationship, but this time I said goodbye for the last time. Immediately I resumed daily drinking. I began frequenting gay bars.

It was early 1984; one Friday night I met a woman in a bar whom I found very attractive and we started a conversation. We danced and had a few drinks together. I invited her to my apartment. When she refused, I got mad and stormed out of the bar. She did not have a car, so I literally left her high and dry. I don't know how she got home, and I don't even recall her name. In my drunken, selfish stupor, I walked out on her and went home. The next day I woke up with the grandfather of all hangovers. After somehow making it through the day, I went to bed and woke up the second day, still hung over. This had never happened in my life before - a two-day hangover! I sat on the edge of the bed, my pounding head in my hands. The first thought that came to me was, "Every time you pick up a drink you're playing with fire. " I thought about it and thought about it. I remembered my alcoholic family; I remembered the courses in alcoholism I had taken at Russell Sage. I was in pain, bewildered and troubled, and I was very much alone. Perhaps my experience as a child of an alcoholic meant I needed some help from other ACOAs, and so it was that I began to attend Al Anon meetings. Al Anon is a fellowship of friends and relatives of alcoholics. I was ready to admit that I was the adult child of an alcoholic, so I went to several meetings, and then one night, as I sat listening to a speaker at a meeting, it suddenly hit me like a punch in the gut: This was *my problem. I am* an alcoholic. Oh, my God, I thought, how could this be? How could this unfailing friend, alcohol, be my worst enemy? How could the dear friend who was there for me in every circumstance be against me? How could the very thing I counted on in good times and bad not be good for me? How could my life have been such a terrible disaster just because of *drinking*?

It was a blow to my ego. It was a horrendous truth. It was a shocking awareness. It was a deeply painful admission. It was an undeniable truth. I began attending Alcoholics Anonymous meetings, found a sponsor and went to 90 meetings in 90 days, the practice recommended to new members. When I asked my first sponsor if she thought I was really an alcoholic, she reminded me that if I had left my entire family due to my drinking behavior it was an "alcoholic bottom" and I was on my way to another one if I didn't stop drinking. It made sense to me and I was very grateful it did, that I stopped drinking and that Cathy was my first and invaluable sponsor. I had met her while attending Russell Sage College.

About this time, I met a woman named Rev. Myrtle. She was part Native American, an excellent psychic and a teacher of psychism. I attended several psychic circles in her home. During one of these circles, Jesus the Christ appeared in front of me in a long white robe and holding a large loaf of bread. He said to me, "Lay down your life for me and I will give you the bread of life." It took me several weeks to relate this revelatory message to my drinking problem. One evening as Myrtle and I sat for dinner in a local diner, I ordered a coke instead of a vodka and tonic. Myrtle commended me for it and thanked God that I had finally answered her prayers for my sobriety. My last drink was July 24, 1984. I was 55.

In those early months of recovery, I had a deep inner urge to demonstrate to God my intention to stop drinking and change my life. Something inside me longed to show outwardly to God that I wanted to accept responsibility for my life and seek a sober life. Although I was raised in a Protestant home, I went on my lunch hours to a nearby Catholic Church and prayed. I saw for the first time the Stations of the Cross depicted by frescos on the walls of the sanctuary. I heard about the Auriesville Shrine, a martyr's shrine just west of Amsterdam, New York, and traveled there frequently to walk the outdoor Stations of the Cross, sometimes carrying one of the small wooden crosses provided.

I desired to know more about God and directed my attention to the Bible. I recalled those rare times when my mother quoted Scripture. She mentioned Hebrews 2:6: *What is man that thou art mindful of him? or the son of man, that thou visitest him? Thou madest him a little lower than the angels.* I also recalled the stained glass window at the First Universalist Church I attended as a child. On it was - and still is - written, *And now abideth faith, hope, and charity, these three; but the greatest of these is charity.* I Cor. 13:13 Rev. Myrtle agreed to be my Bible teacher, and for many months I would pick her up at her home, we would go out for supper and then drive to a river, lake, or pond, where we would sit in my car and read the Bible together, she explaining the lessons. I recorded every session in what I call my "working Bible," full of marginal notes and highlights. We did this from June 1984 to May 1985. We sought out a body of water, which not only provides humans with a calming effect, but also is an excellent transmitter of psychic energy. I bought and read daily a meditation book for recovering alcoholic women, entitled *Each Day a New Beginning*. I have reread it many times since. I relied heavily on my first sponsor during those early months; she was indispensable. She told me to shut up and listen at the meetings, to let her do my thinking until my head was clear enough to do my own. A sponsor is a person in whom you can confide what you are not yet ready to relate to a group. I could share with Cathy, but not a group the fact that I had left my family, that I was a homosexual or that I needed help for my drinking.

In 1984, I had to sit for the comprehensive exam, a prerequisite to graduation from the masters program at Russell Sage. It would cover four years of study. In addition to planning an intensive study review, I sought out Ann Fisher, a local but nationally famous astrologist. She helped others to stop smoking and so I sought her out to help me focus, study and prepare myself mentally for the exam. With the greatest relief and joy, I learned that I had passed it. Still ahead of me was writing the required thesis, for which I found a faculty member to be my monitor. Unable to find a survey form appropriate for my topic, I had to design my own survey, which took a lot of time. I desired to interview members of AA and counselors to get their opinion on the twelve steps of AA. I saw the steps as containing two features: a social aspect and a spiritual aspect. The answers to my questions would define which of the two aspects the target population considered more important. After about eight months of work on the survey, I became quite discouraged and told a friend I was going to quit the master's program. Her response was one of those comments that stick forever in one's memory: "You told me last year that you felt God directed you to take the master's program at Sage; don't you think he intended you to *finish?*" I took the comment to heart and resumed my effort on the thesis. I got a response of nearly 80% to my survey, astounding my monitor. I finally graduated, on May 18, 1986, and Evie, Marty and his wife, Robin and Wendy and Cliff all came to help me celebrate. I had a small gathering in my front yard at home afterward, and the weather was perfect for the occasion.

After graduation, I treated myself to a vacation trip to Los Angeles to visit my niece, Morgan. Then, just days before the trip, I received a telephone call from an administrator at Russell Sage. She called me on Memorial Day, which in itself surprised me. However, a greater surprise was her message. She told me that I had not really graduated because my grade point average was insufficient for graduation. I was enraged. I told her I had the paper in my hand, I had attended the graduation ceremony and I had celebrated with my family. She was adamant. I was livid. It was one of the blackest days of my life - six years of work and struggle. Not to mention all those student loans. Not graduated?

It just so happened (I believe that there *are* no coincidences) that a few weeks earlier I had met a faculty member of the college. I called her and she gave me sage advice for Sage: "Call the Dean of Women and make an appointment," she said, "Do not take your diploma with you but rather a copy of it. If she doesn't rescind the threat tell her that you will go to a civil court with action against Sage." When I arrived to meet the Dean I found that she, too, was a grandmother and we had some light conversation about that common experience. Then she volunteered the information that she had reviewed my transcript and after editing out some of my electives and editing in some of them, my GPA was sufficient for graduation. It was a relief to know that I did not have to follow through on my threat. My degree was secure. Once more, I celebrated my success at Sage.

Although I was working fulltime at Planned Parenthood as their fiscal manager, I had managed somehow to work a six-week internship at the Detoxification Unit of

Samaritan Hospital in Troy as part of the degree program at Russell Sage. It was a challenge to spend the day at the hospital and then put in two or three hours in the evening and Saturday to keep caught up in my accounting job. It was during the short six-week internship at Samaritan that I viewed a poignantly sad scene. After screening a sixteen-year-old boy in the ER as a potential client for the Detox unit, he refused help. His mother begged him, to no avail. I saw him walk away with her. I prayed for him and his well-being as well as for his mother's distress.

In December of 1984 my grandson Michael David was born. Wendy and Cliff now had their first son, Michael. Their first child, Katie Joy had arrived into the world on April 12, my sister Ada's birthday 71 years earlier – the night the Titanic went down on her maiden voyage. Michael was born on Christmas Eve. I made the usual Christmastime trip, and went to see Wendy at Strong Memorial Hospital. Cliff was home with the other children. Although Wendy was supremely happy at the birth of her fourth child, she looked forlorn lying in a hospital bed on this joyous holiday eve. I said goodbye and went down the hall, but thought how sad for her to be alone tonight. I couldn't leave her, so I made a call to cancel a scheduled meeting with a friend, and returned to Wendy's bedside to spend another few hours with her.

Upon my return to home, I responded to an advertisement in the Schenectady Gazette for a part time ed-voc counselor at the day and evening Alcoholism Treatment Center at Ellis Hospital. With the degree in hand, and sobriety my decision, I felt that now I could make another attempt at counseling. The employment office (human resource department, now) agreed and they hired me for 20 daytime hours as an ed-voc counselor and soon there was an opening for a 20-hour evening alcoholism counselor. At last, I worked in my discipline of choice, albeit half of the time was more business oriented than counseling oriented. As an ed-voc counselor, I recommended to some clients that they take an aptitude test to assist them in identifying a suitable course of study. It occurred to me that I ought to take it myself, just to know their experience. Because I was at the cusp between accounting and counseling, my responses to the questions conflicted. So much so that at the summation of the test, when the computer printed out the careers one was likely to succeed in, mine read: "Nothing." I shared it with the clients and we all had a great laugh.

For several evenings, I sat in on group counseling as a co-facilitator. Then one night before I left work, my boss told me that the following evening I would facilitate a group on my own. I began to worry that maybe I was not counselor material after all. The first job had been a disaster. Yet something inside told me I could be a good counselor - or was my ego just egging me on? The next morning I opened the Bible at random, as I had begun to do to remain sober. I opened to read, *Settle it therefore in your hearts, not to meditate before what ye shall answer: For I will give you a mouth and wisdom, which all your adversaries shall not be able to gainsay nor resist.* Luke 21:14-15

It gave me the confidence I needed; it gave me the spiritual support I sought. I went into group that night full of confidence. The exercise that was presented to the group that night was called "lifeboat" in which it was decided who would theoretically remain in the lifeboat made for six but carrying twelve, each described by age, sex and occupation. I facilitated the exercise and presented all the options I could imagine, and then I couldn't think of another track for the discussion to take. I stood there, with sixteen clients, wondering what I should say next and silently asking God. Suddenly the door to the therapy room opened and a fellow counselor brought a new client into the group. Introductions completed, he shared his experiences with that same exercise at another treatment facility. Thus ended the group session.

During my employment at Ellis, I sat for the CAC exam - New York State's Credentialed Alcoholism Counselor. I felt that I had prepared well, but it was a very tough test, including both written and oral segments. I fretted about the outcome, awaiting the results. My boss at Ellis called me to his office. He shook my hand and said he got word that I had passed the exam. I was elated! Some people take the exam more than once before they succeed. In later years, the credential became CASAC (Credentialed Alcohol and Substance Abuse Counselor), since most active alcoholics are dual-addicted. Most had problems with marijuana, cocaine, amphetamines, or other substances. Therefore the existing CAC counselors were grandfathered in to CASACs. I renewed my credential past retirement in the event I got an opportunity to use it as a volunteer or part time counselor. In 1999, I let my bi-annual renewal option lapse, ending my credentialed status.

I had moved from the Stockade section to the Mt. Pleasant section of Schenectady in 1984 to a small cottage with a tiny but sheltered front yard. The kindly landlady was an aged Italian woman who was very friendly and shared the vegetables in her well cared for garden. While I lived there, she died. I went to her viewing hours out of great respect for her, which amazed her children.

About this time, I got a telephone call from Rochester telling me that my brother Al was drinking again. He had relapsed. He was four years older than I was, had already been in and out of Alcoholics Anonymous for years, so it should not have been a surprise. However, this time it hit me hard. Now I was a kindred spirit in the program; now I shared the same struggle for sobriety. I went to work the next morning, thinking I would be okay. As I sat at the morning staff meeting, awaiting the director to join us, I suddenly jumped up and left the room in tears. I went to the secretary and told her to inform the boss I couldn't work that day. I went home and called my AA sponsor; I called my therapist; I looked in my meeting book and found a noon meeting to which I went. I spoke out, crying, that I couldn't stay sober for the whole family. The usual supportive comments came my way - You don't have to! The next day I was back on the job, aware of how vulnerable I now was to the actions of my family, especially as they related to alcoholism.

As the end of 1984 neared, I perused the help wanted ads in the *Schenectady Gazette*, not actively seeking employment, just out of habit. Then my eye caught an ad placed by the NYS Department of Corrections seeking a full time alcoholism counselor with a beginning wage of $30,000, double my salary at the time. I was more curious than excited about the prospect of working in a prison. I sent a resume. Shortly thereafter, I went to a workshop on alcoholism treatment, held at Conifer Park in the Capital District. There I met a young black man who had also applied for the job. Aware that the majority of inmates are black and Hispanic I assumed that he would get the job, so I completely put the idea out of my mind. About two months later, I got a telephone call from the correctional facility in Comstock, asking me if I would come for an interview. I think my jaw dropped in amazement because she repeated her question. We set the appointment and when I told the interviewers that I had decided to become a counselor before I stopped drinking, they laughed aloud. I only had a couple years of recovery, but they hired me. I quickly took a room at a motel near Whitehall and then found an apartment in the village that afforded a short six-mile commute. After a full week of orientation, which explained the rules and regulations of the prison system, I commenced work. My job was to implement the state-designed Alcohol and Substance Abuse Treatment program (ASAT). Inmates signed up for the

12-week program of group counseling. There was always a waiting list, although many signed up merely to impress the parole department upon review. My office was in the minimum-security prison (H block) but I held groups both there and in the medium security facility next door. I called out and screened 30 men at a time. To call out means to present a list to the administrators who then notify the inmates of when and where to show up. I held 16 groups per week, afternoons and evenings. H block consisted of a few buildings. It was the last stop for the inmates prior to release. They could opt to attend classes in the medium security facility, but most inmates did work in the community. Perhaps you have seen correctional vehicles alongside a country road or near a municipal building where green-clothed men paint, clean up litter, etc. - always guarded, of course. My hours were 1:00 pm to 9:00 pm. One of the biggest shocks when I worked at the Comstock prisons was the first time I saw release dates of 2000 and later. It was 1987 and these men would be in prison for at least another fifteen years! Of course, there is a date at which the inmate is reviewed by the Corrections Department to ascertain if he is eligible for parole, and many inmates are freed before they reach that original release date.

This move to Whitehall was a significant change in workplace, home and the AA meetings that I regularly attended. In order to maintain my sobriety I decided to do another 90 meetings in 90 days, as I had done when I first stopped drinking. Every small town has a weekly meeting, so from the meeting book I found and attended various groups. I also decided to locate a counselor to see on a regular basis. Not that I had a "presenting problem" but because now that I was in a new environment with no close friends I thought it would be a good idea to see someone who would spot changes in my behavior or personality, and thereby prevent me from a possible relapse into drinking again.

After I had worked two years on the job, my supervisor asked if I would like to go across the street to work and set up the ASAT program there. Great Meadow, the maximum-security prison, was across the street. Excited about a new challenge, a new population to work with and being entrusted with yet another opportunity to initiate the treatment program all superceded any fears about going through the gate of that ominous-looking building where Al Capone and his gang of the 1930's had been incarcerated.

After three months there, my boss Pat summoned me again and asked if I would return to my prior position and supervise three other counselors. Calling out inmates was not as easy at Great Meadow; for some reason the communication channels between the administrators and I was less than agreeable. It could well be that the correction officers were not happy to see a woman behind the gate, for some reason. So I returned to the prisons across the street to orient and supervise three other counselors in the program. We could offer more counseling groups and it was good to have some peer-level support in my work. Naturally, I had many memorable experiences working in that environment, but a couple of significant comments by inmates during group counseling sessions remain with me. One of them so touched me that I included it in my first book, *The Laughing Christ* (2002). It bears repeating: When questioned by a fellow inmate about how one can stay sober after years of drinking and drugging, the response came quickly and firmly, "You have to fall in love with yourself again."

Another episode is memorable. One afternoon at a group session in H Block an older inmate (about 30, doing his third bid) was asked by a 20 year-old doing his first bid, If you know so much about staying sober, how come you're here doing your third bid? Without hesitation the response came: Because when I was doing my first bid I thought I knew all the answers, just like you! Comments like these from fellow inmates are far more effective in the treatment milieu than all the words of counselors.

The Whitehall apartment proved to be too far away from Albany, where I was attending weekly psychic/spiritual development classes and Sunday evening services at Trinity Temple. I took a first floor flat in Schuylerville, which is about halfway between Comstock and Albany. It was a dark apartment and apparently conducive to squirrel habitation, as one day a squirrel decided to share my bedroom; the landlord built a tray with poison on it and hung it under the hole the culprit used. I think it worked, but I did not, as I recall, stay long enough to find out. After a year, I moved from there to Hudson Falls, closer to Comstock. It was a fine, newly remodeled apartment with two bedrooms and one-and-a-half baths so I could easily put up Marty and his family when they visited me that Thanksgiving. Marty, Robin, and their sons Nick and Shane, and I enjoyed a walk in the nearby woods and watched the Champlain Canal lock in operation.

My sister, Joy, came to visit me in Whitehall and Hudson Falls, a year later. Both times, it was because she wanted to visit Fort Ticonderoga due to her interest in the Revolutionary War. Oddly enough, both times her car broke down in Ticonderoga - and the mechanic remembered her the second time! Both times when Joy came I was in the process of moving, first from Whitehall to Schuylerville and then from Schuylerville to Hudson Falls. While I was living in Whitehall Evie and Owen also came for a visit and we went to the local park and playground and watched the Erie Canal lock in operation. It always delighted me to see the kids and the grandkids. My life style had resulted in me being a grandmother to visit, not a grandmother to be near for babysitting. There were times when I was poignantly aware of this fact. There were times when I thought I could be of some help with the grandchildren, and yet my life seemed to be taking a different direction. I made no apologies because I felt that I was doing what I needed to do with my life at that time.

During my work at the prisons, I never felt threatened by inmates, no matter what the situation was. They always respected me, even the day that there was an uprising in the gym at the medium security prison. Overcrowding of the prison resulted in converting the gym into a temporary dorm building. The inmates did not like it at all; many used the gym regularly for exercise and sports, especially in the winter months. It was about 2:30 pm that day in the gym when a group of prisoners began a noisy disturbance. Corrections Officers came from all over the facility. The morning shift was held over as the second (3-11 pm) shift reported in, doubling the number of Corrections Officers available. I was in the gym building, orienting a new ASAT counselor to the job. Although she was an army veteran, you could tell she was nervous in this setting.

Several officers crowded into the office with us, and one of them turned to me and said that I was a coward not to go out into the population. I could not believe my ears. From the days of orientation onward, my instructions were never to interfere with the COs when they were working. I told him I would be willing to go out and talk to the inmates in an effort to quell the situation. Before I left the office, the official decision came down: get the troublemakers separate from the general population and meet with them in the library to listen to their demands. My job was to talk to the ringleaders and tell them about the plan. I agreed. The inmates listened to me and corrections officers escorted them to the library.

As soon as we arrived in the library, the door was closed and locked. The officers began taking names and numbers, and the result was that all were immediately transferred to maximum-security across the street. Not only were the inmates surprised and very angry, but I was shocked to see this tactic being used, and angry that I had been used by the officers. It was especially painful to behold since one of the inmates taken to the library had not taken part in the uprising. He only joined those led to the library as a gesture of support - but he, too, went to maximum security. I wanted to go see him to explain and even put in a word for him, but I did not. I doubted very strongly that it would help.

Chapter 5: A New Spiritual Adventure

1987-2003 Age 58 to 74

In the fall of 1984, fascinated by the concept of communication between the earth plane and spirit, and having learned that everyone is psychic and can develop that talent, I signed up for a three-year course of study in psychic/spiritual development at Trinity Temple in Albany. The lessons included how to read auras (the energy field which surrounds all humans, indeed all living forms); the energy centers in the body called chakras and their affiliated endocrine glands; the entities who come from the spirit world (angels, guides, teachers, loved ones) to assist and advise us on our spiritual journey. We also learned about the history of psychism in the US that began with the Fox sisters near Palmyra in 1848. We learned how to "tune in" to spirit entities and receive information from them. Spirit communication is a legitimate pursuit and those who are unwilling to accept it only deprive themselves of a rewarding and educational experience. Rev. Penny always emphasized the seriousness of contacting spirit, which is a privilege and a responsibility. It is not to be used as an entertainment venue. Some mediums are born with the natural ability to see spirit (clairvoyance), hear spirit (clairaudience) or to feel the message from spirit (clairsentience). I learned that I am clairsentient. Written exams were taken to test our learning and measure our worthiness to receive certification. The final test consisted of giving several verifiable psychic messages from the church pulpit for two or three consecutive Sundays.

Upon completion of the psychic development classes at Trinity Temple, I became a certified medium, which qualified me to give psychic messages during the service at Trinity. During the summer months, I found myself drawn more and more to the idea of becoming a minister. After the evening service one Sunday in August of 1987, I asked Rev. Penny Donovan if she would train me to be a minister. She quickly agreed; too quickly. There were things about me I felt she should know before enrolling me in the ministry class. I telephoned her and said I would like to meet in person to discuss my enrollment. When we met, I told her that I was divorced, that I was a recovering alcoholic and I told her about my sexual orientation. At each comment, she said that was not a problem. What a relief to know that she was not homophobic and did not see a recovering alcoholic or a gay person as unworthy to serve God. Therefore, a month later, in September of 1987, I began the curriculum leading to ordination as a Christian Metaphysical Minister.

Rev. Penny manifested integrity beyond that of anyone I have ever known before or since. She taught all the ministry classes. Her lessons included rich examples of her own experiences in the ministry, at a time when female ministers were rare. Personally, she is an unassuming, loving, compassionate human being. Professionally, she is a spiritual teacher with a deep and abiding love for Scripture, for God and for Jesus Christ. Her primary goal in life is to pass on Jesus' teachings, to explain Scripture from a metaphysical view and to help people understand that communication with the spirit world has no basis in magic or in evil intent. It is an option anyone can choose who desires to learn.

Entities on the other side help us on our spiritual path. Sincere seekers have always found comfort, assurance and love in such communication. Throughout history, people have believed in spirit communication. (From the sibyls and oracles of ancient Greece to the mediums and psychics of today, prophets and seers are sought by those curious about the future.) Today the difference is that more and more individuals are willing to talk publicly about their belief in psychism and to watch psychics on TV. Believers cannot be dissuaded. Disbelievers will not listen.

As I studied for the ministry, I tried desperately to find a place from which I could commute to Comstock daily and Albany weekly. Thus it was that I moved to Greenwich (pronounced "green witch" by the locals). I resigned from my job at the Comstock prisons and, accepting a huge cut in pay, I took a job in Albany at St. Peter's Addiction Recovery Center (SPARC) as a senior therapist in a halfway house for male alcoholics. The facility also provided day treatment for men and women. In addition to the group counseling sessions there was a daily lecture and all counselors were required to participate. During my tenure there, I asked the director if I could add to the daily lectures the topic of spirituality. After assuring him that my intent was not to proselytize, he allowed it. With approximately 60 clients in treatment on any given day, six counselors held individual and group sessions. Another senior therapist, a nurse, a cook, a maintenance man and a house manager, as well as the director of the program constituted the staff.

Along with the changes in my job, there were also changes in my family. Nineteen eighty-seven saw the birth of my second granddaughter. Evie had remarried in 1986 after divorcing her first husband. On May 6, after another long and difficult labor she delivered Stephanie. I drove to Rochester to welcome her and congratulate Evie, who had found a way to name her baby girl after her father and me: Stephanie Rae-Ellen. On my many trips to Rochester, I stayed with one of my children. I was always welcome and it gave us an opportunity to catch up on the news since my last visit. Of course, there were letters and phone calls in between. Mostly I heard about the significant events in their lives. Sometimes I did not. One day I found out that Marty had broken his leg and had been on crutches for six weeks. By the time I heard of it, he was back on his feet.

September of '87 also brought an invitation. The head of the counseling program at Russell Sage College asked me if I would be interested in presenting a two-day workshop on Spirituality and Recovery. It would constitute 12 of the required workshop hours leading to the CAC credential! As one of my professors, he knew I was a recovering alcoholic, an ordained minister and had received the master's degree in alcohol and substance abuse counseling. I was elated at this opportunity and surprised that it came so quickly on the heels of my graduation. They paid me well. I had done a lot of research regarding alcoholism in Scripture. I found an article "Alcohol Abuse in the Old Testament" by Sheldon Seller in the publication *Alcohol and Alcoholism* Vol. 20 No. 1, pp.69-76, 1985, to which I referred. The group that signed up for the workshop was small but met the minimum number required. When we took our lunch break on the second day I realized that I was running low on notes, and I would be finished with the workshop early. After lunch, I went to the Sage library and browsed through the publications. What a surprise when I saw another article by Sellers: "Alcohol Abuse in the New Testament"! It was just what I needed! I read it, teased out significant facts and presented it after lunch. The workshop ended right on schedule.

On October 25, 1987, my world, my life, and my spiritual path were blessed with an experience that changed my life forever. And I do mean *forever*, not just this lifetime. Mere words are puny tools for this story. Simple letters on a printed page fall far short of properly describing the power of the moment and the magnitude of the message, but words are my only tool here. I sat in the sanctuary of Trinity Temple of the Holy Spirit that Sunday evening as Rev. Penny Donovan read from Scripture. A Bible quotation always preceded her sermon. Upon closing the Bible, she suddenly spoke with a different voice - more emphatic, stronger than her usual thin, feminine voice. The words "Beloveds of God . . ." emanated from her mouth, followed by a sermon of such proportion as to stun everyone there. The voice continued with the message, which in essence was that we are all children of God, made in the image of God which is spirit, and we ought to wake up to that fact and live our lives from the truth of our being. When the talk ended, Rev. Penny reeled and required support to sit down. She looked at the clock and wondered what had happened. Yes, she had channeled spirit entities before; many of us had seen her do that. But never from the pulpit. This time she had been in a total trance, unaware of the words she spoke or the content of her speech.

Some of the congregation rushed up to her, anxious to tell her about the powerful, profound lesson. They suggested that she would be famous and command a lot of money. Rev. Penny said "No, I need to find out what is going on here." Subsequently others approached her to "go public" and commercialize the messages as J. Z. Knight had done in California by channeling a spirit entity named Ramtha. No one knew to whom the voice belonged, and when Rev. Penny returned home, she confronted the unseen entity. A figure in white appeared to her. She told him she had not invited him and wanted to know who he was. Then he reminded Rev. Penny of the words she says before every sermon, which include "may only truth come through me." He told her that he was the Archangel Gabriel and that he brought only truth. She told him there was no way that others would believe she was bringing to them an archangel so he told her to refer to him as Lucas, which means "light," as does "Gabriel."

Rev. Penny met with the Board of Trustees at the church and discussed their options as to whether they desired him to speak there again. They decided that he could come once a month. Hence, the term "Angel

Sunday" became part of the services at Trinity, and every week that Lucas spoke the church filled up. He told us that he would come for 12 years, and he did. Over the course of those glorious years, he told us that 11 other master teachers were then bringing the same message to centers of light all over the world where they were accepted and welcomed. He reminded us that spirit entities had been working with Rev. Penny for 500 years to prepare her for this event, teaching her as she walked her spiritual path. Archangel Gabriel (although for a long time we knew him as Lucas) always answered our questions. He was asked about why we are here, how we got here, where we are heading, the future of the world, homosexuality and many other topics. But he said over and over that the one lesson he brought to us, and which the other eleven teachers brought to earth, was that we are *all* children of God, divine in essence, and need to wake up to that truth and live our lives from the Lord God of our Being. (Everything he told us is available in print or on audiocassette tape or both. See final page of Chapter 6.)

While she was in trance, spirit entities constantly monitored Rev. Penny's body to be sure that it was functioning in a healthy manner. Once Lucas asked for a banana to provide her with immediate energy. In addition to the monthly lectures at Trinity, Lucas also provided daylong seminars at other locations that could seat more that 100 people. Then he advised us he would hold a retreat so the faithful could gather for an entire weekend. Several retreats followed, to the great joy of all the participants. Over time, various sites served for his seminars. Not everyone who heard Lucas accepted his words. Some scoffed, suggesting that Rev. Penny was "putting on a show". No one who truly knew her would ever think so. We valued her for her sincerity and honesty, her desire to teach and to be a spiritual leader.

From October 1987 to July 1991, we, the dedicated students, gathered to hear the eternal truths from Lucas. Then, on July 27, 1991, Lucas presented a seminar entitled "Angels, Earthlings and Aliens." He described the seven archangels, after which I went to the microphone to ask him, "Are you an archangel?" Lucas had always invited questions about any topic he covered. His answer to me was, "Yes, do you know which one?" I stammered, trying to recall the descriptions he had just given us. He saved me from my embarrassment and said, "I am Gabriel, the Announcer of the Ages." The awe and surprise of the audience was tangible. Henceforth we were to address him as Gabriel. He said that he comes to earth every 2,000 years, at the beginning of every age.

I cannot say that we became accustomed to hearing Gabriel. I can only say that we gratefully and devotedly enjoyed the many lessons he brought to us. We never took him for granted. Everyone looked forward to his seminars and lectures. Those who heard him regularly were excited about learning the wisdom of the ages, and being in his presence brought us all a sense of profound peace. Then, in 1995, our blessed sessions took a gigantic leap when Master Jesus came to us. Gabriel had held some question and answer sessions in which he answered questions in lieu of giving a lesson. On December 3, 1995, the soft and gentle sound of yet another entity from spirit emanated from Rev. Penny's vocal chords. One of the students went to the mike and began a series of questions in an effort to identify him. The responses indicated that, unlike Gabriel, he had taken form on earth - many times - before. He said his last incarnation was "about the time of the last turning of the ages." He answered other questions put to him that night and told us to call him The One. Many times Gabriel had told us that another one would come to speak to us, ("There is one to follow me") but never identified him. Eventually we learned that The One was in fact Jesus the Christ. The reader might wonder, as we did, why Jesus the Christ first told us to call him The One. The explanation came: Beloved Woman (meaning Rev. Penny) would not accept the idea that she was qualified to bring forth Jesus the Christ. However, her beloved spiritual teachers convinced her that she was.

Children, and dear readers, truth be told, this book is written primarily to tell you of my spiritual path and how profoundly it was affected by the teachings of Gabriel and Jesus Christ; to explain to you some of the lessons I learned while sitting in their presence. Moreover, to give you some inkling of what it was like to hear the ageless wisdom they imparted to us and the spiritual drive they instilled in us. Later in this book, I will explain the ways in which the teachings of these two heavenly guests changed my life. After two false starts at a manuscript containing Gabriel's and Jesus' teachings, I woke up one morning with this thought: Write to your grandchildren. This, added to the fact that both Wendy and Marty asked me to write my life's story are the reasons I wrote this book.

As the wondrous years with Gabriel and the master unfolded, my worldly life continued.

One manifestation of that continuity was the birth of Shane Christian, in March of 1988, to my son Marty and his wife. I traveled to Rochester yet again to welcome this, my eighth grandchild and sixth grandson into the family. I rarely made it to a baby shower through the years, but when I was earning good money, I always sent a shower gift. Nineteen eighty-eight also saw professional membership and presentations. I joined the New York State Federation of Alcoholism Counselors and presented "Spirituality in Recovery" workshops at NYFAC conferences in Syracuse (1988) and Saratoga Springs (1990). I also presented the same topic in Utica for a small firm of alcoholism counselors who offered training for the CAC exam.

While living in Greenwich I completed the ministry classes that had taken three years of study. I sat for a daylong examination and passed it. The church Board gifted each of us with a stole that we had chosen. On June 2, 1990, Rev. Penny A. Donovan, DD, ordained three fellow students and me. Evie and Wendy both made the trip from Rochester, which overjoyed me. After the ordination ceremony, we had a reception in the basement of the church to celebrate. A bagpiper whom I had hired appeared at the reception and played "Amazing Grace". I asked Evie to take our picture together - the piper, all of seven feet tall with his Scottish headgear and I at five feet two made quite a sight! A dear friend, Bell, took me and my daughters out for dinner that night in Greenwich. It was a joyous celebration.

Let me take some time to tell you about some other joys of my life, my great four-leggeds. First, I will tell you how I acquired my toy poodle, Baby. After hearing Gabriel speak on the power of thought, I found myself on the way to work at the prison one day, saying to myself if I could have any dog in the world, what would I want. I decided that a black, female toy poodle, spayed and at least two years old would be perfect. Evie had owned a toy poodle that her grandmother presented her with years before, and Melody had become a beloved family pet. About two weeks later Mary, a woman at the office of the prison, approached me and said she had a dog to give away. It seems the family had acquired the poodle for their daughters who were now both away at college and the parents didn't have time to care for her. Her name was Baby and she was a black toy poodle, spayed and healthy, but 10 years old. I did not let the age deter me. I said, "I'll take her!" But Mary said I should meet Baby first, so I arranged a visit to her home. The following week I picked Baby up, along with all the items for her care. Later I told Mary that Baby and I were getting along fine. Mary was delighted to learn that Baby not only loved me, but also appreciated some of my favorite foods, like spaghetti and ice cream!

About two months after I got Baby, she and I went for a walk in a nearby woodsy area. As I left the car with Baby leashed, I looked down and saw five tiny kittens. Apparently someone had just abandoned them. I put them in a box in the car and took them home where I put them up in the garage. I bought food and litter for them, but knew I could not keep them. I was happy to have my dog. Besides, I was not into cats. If you recall my black cat stories earlier, you can understand why. I tried unsuccessfully, at work, church and in the neighborhood, to place the kitties. Finally, I decided to drop them at a farm nearby. (Later Rev. Penny sternly admonished me for doing so.) As I boxed them up, something told me to keep one. I said to myself that I would not keep a black one. All were black except one, which was gray. I kept her and in the 15 years I have had her she has taught me much. Like focusing on the now, like being still and loving it, like enjoying simple things such as a plastic ball to chase, sunlight on the floor, and quiet music. Smoky has adapted to every new location as she has moved with me. As I write this, she is in her fifth home with me. I wish I could say the same for Baby, my darling toy poodle. The last move she made with me was a very difficult one for her. She had become nearly blind and bumped into the furniture, now placed where she had to identify it and move around it intuitively. Her hearing also failed and when she developed lumps on her breast the vet said he would not do a biopsy and perhaps require two surgeries, which she could not handle at 17. I cried all the way to the vet to have her put down. Yet I like to think that instead I sent her up, because I know I will see her again on the other side. I threw her ashes over the waterfalls near our home in Greenwich, a place where she loved to romp.

On November 4, 1990, her 72nd birthday, my sister Leah died. She had been a ward of the state, a resident of the Rochester State Hospital, for 54 years. Many a year she had not even one visitor, another example of the distance between the members of my birth family. When my children were growing up I used to bring Leah home for Sunday dinner, but during the many years I was away, I didn't see her at all. I don't know if others did.

Reverend Ellen W. Douglas
With beloved toy poodle, Baby
Year of ordination, 1990

I was by now an ordained minister, and the family asked me to officiate at a memorial service for Leah. I agreed, though I had mixed emotions about doing so. I wondered if I could recall the fun I had with her when I was young without crying. In her eulogy, for I was the only one willing to speak, I told of the times when I was a child and she had carried me on her back, piggyback style, and played games with me.

I always liked the name Leah. Leah was the only one in the family whose first given name was in the Bible. In the Old Testament she was the elder daughter of Laban and the sister of Rachel. Adah is in Scripture but my parents settled for Ada. Only a few family members attended the service. Jean, my niece, arranged for Leah's interment in the family plot, next to our father, in Mt. Hope Cemetery.

In late 1990, I moved yet again, from Greenwich to Lansingburgh, north of Troy. I had asked the angels for a freestanding home, inexpensive and near Albany now that I was working in that city. The angels had found for me the freestanding homes I had in Schenectady and Greenwich. For the other places I found to live in, I had not sought angelic help, resulting in homes that were less than desirable. The angels located an inexpensive house trailer, and the owner allowed me to bring my dog and my cat. It was in Lansingburgh, close to Albany thanks to the Interstate nearby. When Evie and Wendy came to visit me in Lansingburgh, we didn't even go to Albany. We just had nice talks, took a long walk on the trails at Peebles Island, watched videos and ate. We took some good pictures, too!

Because I enjoyed speaking and wanted to present topics on self-esteem, I set up a schedule for myself to lecture at various libraries. The advantage in using libraries is that the space costs nothing but on the other hand, lectures must be free; however, I thought it would provide some good exposure for me. For about a year I lectured in libraries from Greenwich to Amsterdam and from Saratoga Springs to Schenectady. I spoke in six counties to audiences of from one to 15. At the Ballston Spa Library only one person showed up, Janet, a fellow student at Russell Sage. I told her she did not need to stay, but she suggested that I give my talk as though there were many people attending. So I did.

Two years later my ninth and last grandchild, Jillian Joy, came into the world. Marty and Robin had their third child and first daughter. I traveled to Rochester for Jillian's birth. It was 1992, the same year in which hurricane Andrew wreaked so much havoc in southern Florida, and also the year Rev. Penny asked me to serve as Assistant Pastor at Trinity Temple. I was thrilled with the idea and she set up a system whereby we alternated in giving the Sunday sermons.

I worked at St. Peter's Addiction Recovery Center until April 1, 1994 at which time I retired. I was 65 and I had worked since I was 14 - earlier, if I count the farm work I did in my 12th and 13th summers - picking cherries and de-tasseling corn. I was active in the church helping out Rev. Penny in any way I could. I began teaching psychic development classes. Shortly after I was ordained, I got it in my head that God must want me to be a chaplain in the NYS Corrections Department. After all, I now was ordained and I had three years of experience working inside the walls. So sure of myself was I in this decision that I invested in several clergy shirts in the belief I would be wearing one every working day. I applied for the job of Chaplain and received a letter from the New York State Council of Churches stating that the Council assists the State of New York "in its efforts to maintain a professional competent chaplainry ministry, by providing certification for Protestant Chaplains". The Council required a processing fee, completion of a long written questionnaire and a copy of my ordination certificate. I then received a letter instructing me to appear for an oral examination in New York City. I took the oral exam, given by seven members of the Council, in September of 1990. Only minutes after the completion of the oral exam, I received the good news: I qualified and received a certification by them. Upon receipt of it, I proudly had it framed. Forthwith I applied for a job as chaplain in the correctional system, only to learn that the department had let go most of the chaplains and was hiring lay people for the task! I was keenly disappointed but startlingly reminded that we can plan as we will, but our plans do not always fit with what God knows is for our highest good.

When I turned 65, on December 26, 1993, I applied for Social Security and because of being married for more than ten years I was eligible to receive benefits based on Steve's income, which came to about $200. per month more than my own income would have provided. At one of the many visits I made to other psychics, I asked if Steve had any comments from the other side. I knew that spirit entities will not come to earthlings unless they choose to, but he did come to her and say, "Tell her to take the money and run; I can't use it." The words and inflection were typically Steve's. My coworkers threw a retirement party for me on April 1, 1994. As a member of AA, I quickly decided to do another 90 meetings in 90 days. I felt that the vigilance I required to maintain sobriety demanded that I repeat the 90 in 90 that I had first done when I stopped drinking. It also brought me into contact with many other recovering individuals; a strong support system needed in recovery.

Soon after I retired, I attended a Board of Trustees meeting at Trinity, of which I now was a member. When new business came up Rev. Penny announced that she wanted me to serve as full-time pastor so she could devote her time to channeling and writing the messages from Archangel Gabriel. I could not believe what I was hearing. I said "Penny, you didn't even warn me!" She said, "I knew you would give me an argument." I was greatly comforted when the Board unanimously supported her, and I became the pastor of Trinity Temple.

For two years, I served as pastor at Trinity Temple. I believed it was my place for the rest of my life. How wrong I was. I could go into detail about the circumstances that preceded my departure from Trinity, but it would serve no purpose to make people look like my adversaries who are still very good friends. From a metaphysical perspective, it was meant to be. It was time to move on in my life, although I didn't see it at the time. Both Rev. Penny and I were advised by Gabriel that it was time to leave Trinity. He knew something we did not, of course. He knew that there was a faction that desired to "take over" the church. God willing it will someday become the beacon of light it was for many years. Gabriel also knew that Rev. Penny and I had significant spiritual work ahead of us. The Board of Directors at Trinity had presented me with a list of concessions, most but not all of which I could agree to. They also offered me a raise in salary. There were offers and counter offers, but finally I resigned. I will not dwell on the disappointment I felt, because I did not have Gabriel's awareness of what was going on "in the wings" so to speak.

Author sitting on Canandaigua City Pier, 1981

Newly elected Pastor of Trinity Temple of the Holy Spirit Albany, NY. 1994

It took me several weeks to recuperate from the shock. Under the new Board, which had taken over, even Archangel Gabriel was not welcome at the church anymore. Thus, I was in good company that evening on August 4, 1996 when Rev. Penny and I both said farewell to our beloved Trinity Temple of the Holy Spirit. Gabriel also gave a brief speech of farewell. It was a reminder of what Gabriel had told us: God gives us all free choice with which angels cannot interfere. He was aware that Penny and I had much work to do and we could accomplish it better elsewhere.

At the time I was guest speaking at the Capital District Church of Religious Science, at the request of a coworker at SPARC. Thus, I began giving guest sermons at CDCRS in 1994. Nevertheless, Trinity was my beloved church home then and I could hardly imagine life without it after eleven memorable years that included the presentations of Archangel Gabriel and Jesus Christ. I had become very comfortable in the pulpit, the congregation seemed to love me, and I had established myself as a local author of sorts. From March 1996 to January of 1999, six columns I wrote appeared in the Religion section of the Saturday edition of *Albany Times Union*.

In September, 1996, when I learned that the Capital District Church of Religious Science was seeking a pastor, I applied for and got the job - on the condition that I travel to California to a national convention of ANTA, a group of New Thought churches which CRS had recently joined. It was a timely and very welcome invitation, so I made the trip to the conference in the San Gabriel Mountains. A friend of mine, Rev. Duane Wood, drove me to the Albany International Airport for the trip, and dropped me off. I told him there was no need to park the car and stay with me. When I approached the ticket counter, I was asked for a picture ID. I had left my driver's license at home because I knew I wasn't going to be driving in California, and arrangements had been made to get me to the conference from San Diego, where I would spend one night with my niece, Morgan. I asked for the supervisor, who declared that the picture ID was a federal law and no way could I board the plane without it. Frantic, and with only about 40 minutes to flight time, I ran out of the airport in search of a cab. I spotted one and asked the driver if she could take me to Troy and back in 40 minutes. She said she could; and she did. With her knowledge of streets, she showed me a new way to my home! I did make the flight on time, but the reason I'm telling this story is to emphasize the point that everything happens for a reason. The female cabbie, as we rode, told me her husband died a year before and she could not get over her grief. I suggested to her that grief is a process, not an event. That it consists of various stages through which one must pass to come to the final acceptance. She seemed greatly relieved and asked where my church was and when it met. I never saw her at the church, but I knew that somehow we needed each other that day. The trip to the San Gabriel Mountains offered a spectacular view from 4,000 feet! We passed a high school which was appropriately named "Top of the World High School."

It was during my first year as pastor at the Capital District Church of Religious Science that I met Genevieve who had just moved from Rhode Island to live with her daughter in Waterford, near Albany. She had telephoned the church for information and told me that she could not drive. I went to see her and we became fast friends, sharing stories about our children and grandchildren. I promised her a ride to church every Sunday. We both had read Science of Mind, the seminal work of Ernest Holmes, who had founded the Church of Religious Science. We had great times together traveling to and from church services and oftentimes took a leisurely ride in the country. Her last years were lived in an assisted living facility in Waterford, near her daughter. I visited her frequently when I lived in Cohoes and at times we ate at the

International House of Pancakes in Albany where Gen enjoyed her favorite meal, strawberry blintzes.

While living in Rhode Island she had been declared legally blind and attended a school for the blind, learning a manual skill. She had made a small footstool, which she generously gave me one day when I told her I was seeking one in a furniture store. I continue to use it daily. When I opened my own business, The Penultimate Sanctuary, she presented me with a solid brass business card holder, which I will always cherish. Another time she gave me a copy of the Concordance of *A Course in Miracles*. She shared my love for the Course and we had attended many discussion groups which focused on its teaching.

Months later, when I decided to leave Albany and return to the Rochester area, I visited Gen in Waterford and told her it would be hard to leave her when we were such good friends, but she said she understood. She had stuck by me through all the months of The Penultimate Sanctuary, never missing a class until the last few months. Before every class, she took me out for supper. Her generosity was unlimited and her devotion to me, my work and my writing were indefatigable. When I opened The Penultimate Sanctuary, she announced that she would tithe to me since she was not attending a church. She left the Church of Religious Science when I was let go by the Board. Tithing had been a long-standing habit with her ever since she had joined the Unity Church years before.

I will never forget her. One especially significant evening in the winter of 1999-2000 I picked up Gen to travel to E. Greenbush for scheduled lecture. It was snowing hard, but when I called her, she said if I was going, she would go. We got to a restaurant en route for supper, but when we came out the falling snow had become a storm and I said to Gen, "Who's going to come out to hear me in this?" And so I took her home. It was a stunning example of her devotion to me. I thought about her with poignancy as my belongings were packed in the U-Haul and as the road to Livonia Center stretched ahead of me.

It was September, 2004, while I was working on this manuscript that I learned Genevieve had left this world to return to God. I arranged a memorial service for her in Albany where eleven of us joined together to celebrate her life, her wit, her intellect, the joy of knowing her. I look forward to seeing her again when I pass on.

There were those who could not attend a Church of Religious Science but who, like Genevieve, thirsted for spiritual knowledge. One such individual was Flavio, a resident of Buenos Aires who wanted to know more about the church. He had gone to the US Embassy in Buenos Aires to find an address to write for information about the denomination. I imagine that Albany, New York was the first listing so the Embassy supplied him with our church's address. We mailed him a copy of Holmes' *Science of Mind,* the seminal teaching of the church, and I found a pen pal in the church to write to him regularly. I have always admired his ingenuity in seeking information he desired from the US Embassy. This is a perfect example of God leading us to that source our heart desires to find. We still communicate, Flavio and I, and perhaps one day his dream to visit the US will be realized.

While vacationing in 1996 at Stonington, Maine, a favorite place of retreat for me, I visited the local bookstore and found a fascinating book entitled *The Lost Years of Jesus.* It would be another year before Gabriel described some of Jesus' previous incarnations, but I had already heard about Jesus' past lives. Moreover, it would be another two years before I decided to write my first book, *The Laughing Christ.* Two experiences impelled me to write it: Archangel

Gabriel's teachings and the reading of many apocryphal books that the early church fathers omitted from the official canon of the church centuries ago. At his final presentation when Gabriel said goodbye to approximately 200 students in Latham, New York, a suburb of Albany, I sat next to a woman who had attended Trinity Temple. Joan turned to me and said she heard I was writing a book about the Master. When I confirmed it, she offered to proofread it for me. I told her when the manuscript was ready I would be in touch to discuss her fee. She came back with, "You don't understand. I would be happy to offer my time freely in exchange for the privilege of being the first to read the book!" Another Gabriel student, Vincenza, whom I had met at Trinity Temple, offered to edit *The Laughing Christ* for me. Vincenza has been a dear and devoted friend for many years now. She also generously edited this book. How blessed I am to have her in my life. I began writing *The Laughing Christ* in 1998 and continued for four years. I give my deep and abiding gratitude to those two wonderful women who offered to assist me because of their affection for me and my writing, their devotion to Gabriel, and their enthusiasm for the tasks they offered to perform.

In October of 1998 I learned that my brother Al had passed into spirit. He had lived in a nursing home several months and then was transferred to a hospital, where he finally passed into spirit. He was only four years older than I, a chronic alcoholic who just could never keep sober for any significant length of time. By his own admission, he told me that he had worked a total of four years in his whole life. A few days before he passed I had visited him. Although he was in a coma I softly said to him that I forgave him, that he had done what he came to do and he ought to go toward the light, for all would be okay. It was necessary for me to say I forgave him, because for many years I had been very angry with him because of all the incessant teasing he had inflicted on me.

The following year, 1999, brought sad news of another sibling. My sister Joy had died. She was my friend, my teacher in mothering and a role model for life. She had been sick for some time, surviving major surgeries until the last. I deeply grieved her passing. I was very close to Joy and we had shared much of our lives, experiences, opinions and fun times. It was a poignant loss which only time would alleviate. When her daughters contacted me to officiate at her funeral, I thought to myself how could I do this? I hesitated briefly then recalled something Gabriel told us, When you are asked to do something it is because you are *able* to do it.

My nieces, Jean and Ruth, wanted me there for reasons of their own and I would have to somehow set aside my own grief to be there for them in their hour of loss. I agreed to be there for the family. It was March and a record snowstorm had dropped 46 inches of snow one day and 22 inches the next. Two exits of the New York State Thruway closed to traffic. Because of the weather, I was surprised but very grateful when two rooms at the funeral home filled with family and friends to honor that fine life Joy lived. Many people gave eulogies, including two daughters-in-law, which in itself speaks very highly of Joy's popularity. She was caring, generous, and supportive of friends. She had raised six children with the same honesty and integrity with which she lived her life. When her children were grown, she worked in a union job in downtown Rochester. She was a staunch union supporter, as was I. After all, I had lived 22 years with a union man, deriving all the benefits gleaned from the union's efforts. At one time, Joy was the president of a local union and her daughter Jean was the president of another local union. This combination was rare and a union paper wrote up the story. Joy was the historian of the family and now she was gone. Mertice and I were the only ones left now. I held up well for the funeral but the return trip to Albany seemed endless. I recalled our good times together instead of the funeral rite. At Joy's request, her ashes were scattered on a lake in the Adirondacks where her family had often vacationed.

The sadness at the loss of my siblings was followed by a professional sadness. In July of 1999, the Board of Trustees at the Church of Religious Science asked me to step down. Here we go again! I believe that my sermons had contained a little too much of Gabriel's teachings which they were not yet ready to accept although I felt the church's dogma was very similar to his lessons. Although I never used Gabriel's name in my sermons, I would sometimes say a great spiritual teacher told me - and some of the congregation were well aware that I spoke of Gabriel, as they had attended Trinity Temple themselves to hear him speak. However, this time it took me only 24 hours to accept the dismissal. Now I finally got the message: I didn't need to be a pastor to be a spiritual teacher! Now I could see that God had something else in mind for me. His intention is not for me to be a pastor. Based on Gabriel's teachings I came to believe that life is not about religion, anyhow. It is not necessary to adhere to a specific dogma of faith; it is essential to understand that we are all children of God and we are all on our way back home to God. Life is about awakening to our own spirituality - our individual spiritual connection to the One Creator God. I used to have a bumper sticker on my car that read, "God is too big for any one religion". Gabriel clearly stated that all religions have some truth but no religion has all truth. However, my friend Gen was very upset about the Board's decision and she refused to return for their Sunday services. She was devoted to me, and showed it constantly in the ensuing months. Although I assured her that I would be happy to get her to the church service on Sundays, she was adamant.

Upon deciding that spirituality is the key to spiritual growth rather than is any specific religious denomination, I applied for an assumed name certificate in July of 1999 and began classes in September. I called my enterprise The Penultimate Sanctuary. My son Roy introduced me to the word "penultimate" a few years earlier when he used it in our conversation. I asked him what it meant and he said next to last, or second last. Since the ultimate sanctuary is one's self being with God, I would offer to *teach people spirituality* (the same initials as my business name). I decided to offer a series of weekly lectures on spirituality at one location that I rented in E. Greenbush, and a weekly group for spirituality discussions at another location, in Latham. The first series thrived for about a month and then died off as people dropped away. However, the group in Latham, consisting of six faithful students, continued to thrive for more than three years. In that time, I wrote and presented over 80 topics, including many reviews of books.

All of the topics were not spiritual topics, but we were a spiritual group, grounded in a common faith and willing to share our spiritual paths with each other on a weekly basis. After the first year, I found a dozen local guest speakers who were willing to come free of charge and tell the group about their areas of expertise. One guest speaker came three separate times to teach us. Mary Lee-Civalier presented one class on Qi Gong energy, an ancient Chinese use of the body's energy. Another time she explained Chinese astrology and the third time she gave an overview of Feng Shui. Vickie explained the various crystals and gems and their value in healing and energy. An intuitive artist created a portrait of me in class. It is a rendering of my physical form with various colors in and around my body. The class watched the artist work. It hangs, framed, in my apartment. Three nurses gave therapeutic massage to everyone in the class. Neil demonstrated polarity therapy. All the guests enjoyed working with and teaching my group. Moreover, the members of the class were very appreciative. Guest speakers gave me a little breather once a month and I too enjoyed learning. I still do some of the Qi Gong exercises every morning.

We were a happy group. We shared our spiritual paths with each other and took every opportunity to celebrate! Christmas, Easter, class year endings in the spring all prompted us to have a potluck social. Summers we had no classes because of vacations. New people would attend occasionally but would not find in the group what they were seeking and so it was, but the original six stayed on. Half were over 60 and half were under 50, all females. It was an excellent example of inter-generational spiritual sharing. As I wrote chapters for my book *The Laughing Christ*, I asked the women in TPS if they would be willing to read a portion of it and give me their comments. They willingly did so and I gleaned valuable input that enabled me to produce a completed work of which we were all proud.

The next task was to publish the book. After receiving several rejection letters from publishers, I decided to self-publish *The Laughing Christ*. To generate the necessary funds to do so I wrote to all the people I knew - friends, acquaintances, business connections. Upon receiving my letter for advance orders and advance payments of my book, nearly 100 people responded. I ordered my first 140 copies and held a publication party. Tina Edwards, a friend, had a cake made specially for the occasion and she brought all the, paper goods and multi-colored balloons. Others provided a variety of dishes to pass. My daughter Wendy came with her husband Cliff. They set up a card table in the front yard to hold the many books that I would sign, as the advance orders were filled. About 40 people came, and I mailed signed copies to those who could not get to the party. Then I placed ads in some monthly magazines and sold another hundred copies of the book. I gave several copies away until a friend, Lois, advised me to stop doing so because it cost too much. She recommended that I give away bookmarks instead and Joe, another dear friend, designed and printed them for me. At this writing, I have sold, given away or bartered nearly 420 copies of *The Laughing Christ.* I am a firm believer in bartering and I bartered copies of my book with my hairdresser, the lady from whom I bought my produce, my mechanic, my website host and my massage therapist. While writing this book I bartered copies of *The Laughing Christ* for a book and a Christmas gift.

Albany was not only the place where I discovered Gabriel and his teachings and saw my first book published. It was also the occasion of publicly affirming and acknowledging myself in the gay community. The director of the Capital District gay center on Hudson Avenue called me one day in 2001. She asked me to be a marshal in the Gay Pride Parade for the city of Albany. I had recently attended some presentations to the senior members of the gay center and had met her there. Her intention was to have all the generations represented to indicate the generational composition of gays and lesbians in the area. I was delighted to accept. It was my first opportunity to go public with my homosexuality, to come out of the closet to the world. I decided it was time. I was 72. A student at Albany High School represented the youngest generation, and a member of the Gay Pride Agenda (a political group) in New York City completed the trio of marshals. The day of the parade was rainy, but the crowd that came out had a joyous time. We marshals rode in a two-horse drawn carriage through southeast Albany, ending in Washington Park for a picnic, which included prizes to the best parade floats. The parade was covered by one of the local TV channels that evening, and I have pictures taken by friends of that honored event.

While living in eastern New York State I had two
relationships, both with women living far away (one in
Vermont and another in Massachusetts). Long distance
relationships are difficult to maintain and they both
ended because of an unwillingness of both parties to
make a commitment to relocate. The reason I have
not included more stories about my homosexuality is
that I have never identified myself primarily with my
sexual orientation. Perhaps that is because I never
lived with a partner. Some periods of my life were
years of survival, others were years of spiritual
seeking, seeking, and seeking. I wanted to know the
answers to age-old questions of Why am I here, What
is life all about? Where am I going? When I heard
Archangel Gabriel answer all these questions for me, I
became an avid listener, an eager student. When
Gabriel left, I dedicated myself to teaching others
what I had learned. My primary purpose in life now is
to spread the word about our sacred nature, our
reason for being on planet Earth at this time, the
lessons we must learn. It is time that we accepted our
own divinity, realized perfect health as ordained by
God and came to understand that the kingdom of God
is within, not merely a place "out there somewhere"
for us to go to upon our demise.

On my spiritual journey I met other individuals bent
on providing spiritual fellowship and teaching
spirituality. A mutual friend introduced me to Rev.
Doris Pratt of Germantown, in the mid-Hudson area.
At her enterprise, Life Center for Metaphysics, I
presented several lectures to a small but enthusiastic
group.

That same year, 2000, as autumn approached, I felt it
was also autumn for the Penultimate Sanctuary. It
was time to end my weekly presentations. I had
offered a multitude of topics, and presented a dozen
guest speakers. We had occupied three different
locations in three years. The angels always found a
place for us to meet. In December we had a glorious

159

celebration to acknowledge our mutual joy of these three years. I hope that the lessons brought us a little closer to our Ultimate Sanctuary - the Presence of God.

It was not long after the holidays that I began to think about moving back to my home area. Something had always kept me away - a relationship, college, jobs, Trinity Temple classes, Archangel Gabriel, serving as pastor at two churches, The Penultimate Sanctuary. I had accomplished all the things that had kept me in the Albany area for 26 years. In February of 2003, I decided to move back to Rochester and informed my children. They were pleased with my decision. Evie, Marty, Wendy and her husband Cliff plus my grandson, Michael, came to load up the U-Haul. Darryl and Don, dear friends and followers of Gabriel, came to help also. The week before my move, Don had brought and installed a brand new computer tower to upgrade my old 386 system. I told him it was an extremely generous gift. He said in effect that he himself was not a writer or a speaker, but he wanted to support me in those talents. The children drove the van back to Rochester and moved me into my new apartment in Livonia Center.

I must tell you about that journey westward to my new home. My only concern about the trip was the effect it would have on Smoky. Days prior to the move, I consulted the vet and he gave me a tranquillizer to crush and mix in Smoky's food an hour or two before leaving. I prepared the concoction but she refused to eat it. I was apprehensive about the trip. She would be safe enough in her cage, but I knew I was in for a lot of loud complaining. She didn't even like the trip to the vet a few blocks away and complained all the way. The four-hour trip was exacerbated by an accident that brought all three of our vehicles to a dead stop on the NYS Thruway! The first couple of hours I listened to Smoky and quietly spoke to her in calming tones, saying you are fine, we

are well, you are all right, etc. When we became
stalled, she continued to cry. I lost my temper and
yelled at her, telling her I'd had enough and I wasn't
going listen to her keep up. Well, her response to my
harangue was a deep, deep growl, the likes of which I
had never heard come from her vocal chords. I
couldn't help but laugh at her. It was as though she
was saying you think these sounds were bad, listen to
this!

My beloved Smokey at 13 y.o.a.
Sunning herself in Cohoes, NY

Chapter 6: My Senior Years

2003 on; age 74 on

Now, dear children, dear grandchildren, dear readers, this final chapter of my life's story begins with my move from Cohoes to Livonia Center, New York. Just prior to leaving Cohoes, I got a telephone call from Unity in the Southern Tier in Endicott, New York, asking if I would be a guest speaker. Although it would mean driving over two hours each way, I agreed because I sorely missed the speaking engagements. However, I wanted to complete my move before presenting a sermon there. Interestingly enough, the distance to Endicott from Albany and from my new home are almost the same.

As I contemplated my move I considered the fact that my granddaughter Katie was expecting her first child. She had met and married a fellow cadet at an Air Force base in Texas. I had planned to move in September, but her baby was due about that time and I didn't want my move to compete with her delivery. So I began my search for living quarters near Rochester in June. I sought another freestanding home of my own to rent. It mattered little whether it was a mobile home or a small cottage such as I had in Cohoes. Living in Rochester was not an option. With all the kids south of Routes 5 and 20, I knew the best location would be somewhere between Avon and Canandaigua, between Henrietta and Mt. Morris. Originally, I thought of the village of Canandaigua, because I had become familiar with it in all our commutes to the cottage, I desired to be near water and it wasn't far from Evie. Then my thoughts shifted and I decided on living closer to Wendy, in Avon, and Marty, in Lima. Two things became problematic: (1) the cost of living was higher in the Rochester area (which I had anticipated) meaning rental property would be more expensive and (2) nearly all the ads for rentals forbade pets. No way was I going to give up my beloved Smoky.

Prior to seeking a new residence, I asked the angels to locate a new home for me. In the years before, when I asked, I had found a perfect home. When I went fiercely ahead with my own ideas the choices were less than desirable. I looked at two other places in June as I visited the area of northern Livingston County, and on my next trip, in July 2003, I saw the apartment I now live in, a remodeled rural Catholic Church, complete with steeple and cross! My new home is a spacious one-bedroom apartment beautifully decorated with lilac trim which enhances the stained-glass windows. Here, indeed, I can easily feel the Presence of God. Sometimes I sing to myself the short hymn that we sing at Unity in the Southern Tier, "Surely the Presence of the Lord is in this place." Everyone who visits me speaks highly of my home, for it is lovely to the eye. In addition to its physical beauty, I believe that the vibrations are strongly positive and sacred due to the years of singing and praising God, of praying and worshiping the Creator. Someone once said of hymns, "He who sings praises twice."

As I mentioned earlier, three of my children traveled to Cohoes, packed the U-Haul I had rented and drove it to my new home. The night before the move was a memorable time. Evie and Wendy slept in a tent which took up most of my little front yard. Cliff, Marty and Michael slept in the house, on the couch and on the floor. I kept my own bed. There were comments back and forth, in and out of the house, until we all finally settled down for a good sleep. Marty, with experience packing U-Hauls, supervised the move the next day. He wasn't sure he could fit all the furniture in, but he did. Upon arrival in Livonia, with the help of my grandson Michael and his friends, my furniture was in by suppertime on August 2, 2003.

I knew that I was leaving a large support system in the Capital District, so yet again in my nomadic life of recent years, I found myself in a position where I had to build a new group of friends. Telephone calls are no longer toll calls now to keep in touch with my children and grandchildren and I am more readily available for special events in their lives. Although my children are now closer - two within ten miles and the other two within 40 miles - they have their lives to live and I do not expect to have them drop in frequently. Moreover, my family is not interested in my particular spiritual beliefs or the wondrous lessons I learned from Archangel Gabriel. Perhaps one day they will be.

In an effort to begin building a support system I placed an ad in the local weekly to draw people to a discussion group for *A Course in Miracles* to supplant the group I had in Cohoes. Five weeks after moving in, we began the group with five members and me. I also advertised myself as an ordained minister, available for non-denominational weddings. Then I sought a part time job to replace the income I had earned in Cohoes distributing *Wisdom* magazine in the Capital District (Albany, Troy, Schenectady) in order to supplement my Social Security income. I found a part time (4 hours per week) bookkeeping job in downtown Rochester. Everything was falling into place, confirming for me that it was a good move.

My timing had been perfect, for six weeks later, on September 24, Katie Erwin delivered her baby girl and named her Kylee Joy. She and Brandon proudly announced her arrival and Wendy flew to Texas to welcome her new granddaughter into the world. The unfolding weeks and months have convinced me that my move was timely. I see the boys frequently, and Wendy and Evie keep in touch regularly, taking an interest in what I do, where I go and whom I meet. We live separate lives and have diverse ideas about religion and politics, but we get along very well, spend time together every few days and phone in between.

It is not a daily contact but sufficient for us. I know they are there if I need them, as of course are my sons. At this point I would like to make mention of a comment I made to my dear friend and editor of this book about my surprise that my kids still love me. "Why wouldn't they?" she asked. I said, "Because I walked out on them when they were teenagers. I guess it shows how much I have grown." Her instantaneous response startled me. She said, "It shows how much **they** have grown." It was a moment of awareness that stunned and then pleased me. Thank you, Vincy, for your keen observation. And thank you, children, for forgiving me and loving me in spite of my past behavior.

Moving back to Rochester also enabled me to visit my only living sibling, Mertice, who then resided at St. Ann's Nursing Home. Mertice's two daughters live out of state, but kept in touch with Wayne their brother to monitor Mertice's condition. Wayne visited her often, called her every day, and became fully involved in her care by attending family meetings with the nursing home staff. On February 24, 2004, she passed into spirit. It was a true blessing because she had reached the late stage of Parkinson's disease. Although we had grown apart in later years, I had sweet memories of the years when we shared a home while her husband was serving in the Air Force during World War II. On one of my visits to see Mertice in the summer of 2001 I asked her if she would let me tape her memories of her early years. She agreed and I transcribed the hour and a half tape, sending copies to all her children. When Mertice's children, Julie and Holly, asked me to serve at her memorial service, I decided to read a few paragraphs of her own words; what better way to honor someone's life, I thought. Two other clergy and I officiated at Mertice's funeral service, held at St. Ann's. All three of Mertice's children (Blake, her son, predeceased her nine months earlier) presented meaningful, memorable and sometimes funny stories about Mertice's life and their memories of her. The sanctuary was filled with friends and relatives who gathered to honor her life. Eulogies were also given by some of the staff at St. Ann's who had grown fond of Mertice's personality and wit. Now my last sibling had passed on. Now I was the only one left in the family of this generation. I am confident that they will all be there to welcome me when it is time for me to respond to God's call.

I became settled in through August and September, then in October I gave my first sermon at Unity in the Southern Tier located in Endicott, New York. Right away, I sensed a warm connection between the dedicated congregation and myself. As of this writing, I continue to serve once a month as guest speaker, sharing the podium with other guest speakers until they find a fulltime pastor. The congregation has become a part of my spiritual support system, and I appreciate it. Another way to build a support system in this area has been to attend many meetings of Alcoholics Anonymous. There are dozens of meetings every week within ten miles of me. One of the glories of AA is that wherever you go, we are there, and everyone is welcome. In addition to reaching out to meet people here I have begun writing my third book, as yet untitled. Its content and reason for being written will be disclosed in the Introduction. The estimated publication date is summer, 2006. My days begin with what I call an RPM period: read, pray and meditate. This habit, begun some years ago, sustains me on my spiritual path back home to God.

While doing research for this book, I was reminded by Jean, my niece, about the stone tree my maternal grandfather, a stone mason, had helped create. My mother told me years ago that her father had carved a tree out of stone near Seneca Falls, a monument to Red Jacket, famous Indian orator and Seneca Chief who sought to preserve peace with the US. He was born in 1750. His name derived from the fact that in the Revolutionary War he had taken the jacket off a

British soldier and always wore it thereafter. His Indian name is Go-Ya-Wa-Ta, meaning "he keeps them awake."

I located the stone tree monument on route 89 in Seneca County, on the west side of Cayuga Lake, one of the Finger Lakes. It can be seen from the road at the entrance to Canoga Cemetery. The tree stands about 14 feet tall, and stands on a huge rock, surrounded by six stones. The stones bear the names of the six tribes of the Seneca Nation. In my research I learned that a group of volunteers led by Emerson Moran spent several hours in 1987 cleaning up the area which had become so overgrown that the monument was not visible from the road. It was my intention to find my grandfather's name, Thomas Armstrong, as the mason who chiseled that fine monument, but to no avail. He apparently worked for Littlejohn and I suppose many men worked on the construction of the monument that was commissioned in 1891. According to *A History of the Village of Waterloo* (p. 481):

> "For years Maj. Fred H. Furniss was interested in erecting a monument near the birthplace of Red Jacket . . . In October, 1890, he received a letter from one Martha M. Huyler, of New York City, who made a proposition to help in erecting such a monument . . . A fair was held in the Academy of Music in December of 1890, at which $1479.10 was cleared. A contract was made with W. & J. Littlejohn, of Seneca Falls . . ."

168

On page 294 of the same book:

"The ceremonies of the
unveiling of the Red Jacket
monument erected near
Canoga by the Waterloo
Library and Historical Society
were held Wednesday, Oct.
14, 1891 . . . an oration
[was given] by William C.
Bryant, Esq., of Buffalo,
famous for his knowledge of
Indian lore and of the life
and times of Red Jacket . . .
A delegation of Iroquois
Indians from Canada under
leadership of John Buck, the
Fire Keeper, and also a
delegation of Seneca's from
the Cattaraugus reservation,
was present."

It is interesting and heartening to know that my
grandfather played a substantive, creative role in
recording part of the history of our nation and of this
lake country land.

Day of Roy's Wheatland-Chili HS graduation, 1970

Stone tree monument to Red Jacket carved by Thomas Armstrong etal

My personal recording, my own story could not be complete without explaining some of the ways in which Archangel Gabriel's teachings have affected my personal and professional life. First, I would like to say a word directly to my dearly beloved children.

Evie, as first born, you survived all those experimental efforts of our parenting. I see in you some of my own traits: Devotion to others, tenacity in beliefs, and a growing faith in the unseen. You have chosen a rocky road but always bounce back to an upright position and forge ahead with renewed vigor. Your children, Owen and Stephanie, have shown the same independence you have demonstrated, ever since that first day of school when you spurned my offer to walk you there. They, like you, take nothing at face value but rather choose to delve into the details and the truth of a situation. At one time, a psychic advised me that in a past life, you were my daughter and I was your father, an American Indian chief. As the tribe's princess, you were greatly loved and respected. No wonder you value nature in all her glory, flora and fauna alike. Your interest in a moon calendar is probably a reflection of that ancient time.

Roy, you have spent many years of your life as a self-employed excavator. Perhaps your exclusive use of hand tools indicates your respect for Mother Earth and exemplifies your desire to treat her more gently than the huge machines that dig relentlessly into her face. It has pleased me to see you as an avid reader since childhood. Drawn to some great writers, including Nietzsche, (once described as "Prophet of a non-religious religion and an un-philosophical philosophy"), you seem to be ever seeking to learn and to know about life.

Marty, your deep and abiding faith in God is demonstrated in your working life as well as in your familial life. Be proud of the three fine children - Nick,

172

Shane and Jillian - you are raising with your wife, Robin. After building your dream home, you are now dreaming of building the sailboat of your dreams. I look forward to seeing you launch it on its maiden voyage one day and anticipate with joy a sail with you.

Wendy, justly proud mother of Jeff, Bryan, Katie and Mike, and professionally a nurse to the terminally ill, your abiding faith sustains you through all your days. The kudos you have received from patients and survivors in your work with hospice should impress you. With your steadfast and faithful husband, Cliff, you have done a commendable job of parenting your four kids as well as Cliff and Chris, Cliff's children by his first marriage. You both continue to be examples to them of trust, love and peace. As you welcome a new generation into the family, may your children and their children bring you the satisfaction that only parenting can know.

Only love, joy and pride surface when I think of you all. I did not bring you into the world to take care of me, but rather to help you to help yourselves to find your own way. Thus far, you have done exceptionally well. God bless you all on your continuing journey of life.

To all you grandchildren of mine, how very proud I am of you all! Owen, your adventures on the high seas working onboard cruise line ships is a fine opportunity to broaden your horizons, meet people of various countries and cultures, and determine for yourself a career path to follow in the future. Stephanie, I can only say that as you mature you will find motivation and joy in pursuing your unique goals. I wish you the best in every endeavor you undertake. Nick and Mike, having chosen religious colleges to further your education, I am certain you will find your true spiritual path in life. Shane, I wish you the best of success in your final year of high school, including all the extra-curricular activities you choose. You did a fine acting job in the Drama Club last year - maybe Hollywood calls? Jillian, my youngest grandchild, how glad I am to be living near you in order to enjoy your various school celebrations as you continue into the seventh grade and beyond. Jeff, now that you've taken up residence in Brooklyn, with your partner, Anna, I pray that your musical ambition will come to fruition. You have worked hard to make it so. I recently passed on to Stephanie your first CD. (I think the music is more appropriate for your generation.) Bryan, I understand why you have chosen to enter the business world instead of teaching. Not only will you generate a higher income but you will not have to deal with students' behavior. I look forward to your wedding next summer to your beloved, Shanna. Katie Erwin, first of my granddaughters to marry, and mother of my dear great granddaughter Kylee Joy, you are truly a natural for the job. Your gentle motherly instincts are starting Kylee off on a path of love and integrity. Your husband, Brandon, whom I just recently met, has also demonstrated great affection for Kylee. Although I haven't been close to my "adopted" grandchildren, Cliff and Christopher Chapman, I would like to say to you, I'm certain that as you express the qualities of character manifested in your father, Cliff, God will bless you throughout your life. Finally, I take great pleasure in saying that some of my sons-in-law have become like sons to me, enriching my life in these later years.

****

In the closing of this chapter and the book about my life, I present those lessons imparted to us by Archangel Gabriel that most affected my life. They are only a small fraction of the total lessons given to us by Gabriel in those twelve wondrous years. At one time Gabriel told us that our spiritual path is vertical rather than horizontal. We can compile genealogies, and it can be fun, yet our spiritual path is a spiraling journey back to God. Once we were consciously aware of our at-one-ment with God and each other, but in our creative imagination, we decided to descend from the perfection of God to the physical form we take on earth. Our journey back home has begun, but we have a long way to go. We have to wake up to our own divinity. At our own bidding, other lives touch into ours. At our own bidding, others share our lives for a moment or for a lifetime. At our own bidding, we live out the play we ourselves have choreographed, in order that we may learn the lessons we have come to learn. As I now look back at my life as a minister, I perceive a pattern.

One past life that I became aware of took place in the sixth century AD, when I was a young man preaching the lessons Jesus had brought to earth. As a young man, I was killed for heresy. Centuries later, in the 1600s, I came to America with my parents, when I was two. My father was a missionary from Britain, my mother a reluctant passenger on that stormy voyage to America. Later in that lifetime, as a teenager, I wrote down my father's sermons as he dictated them to me, while he channeled the words from spirit. I believe that I admired him and wanted to emulate him, yet women were not allowed into the ministry. It would be another 300 years before my dream would become a reality. As I became an ordained Christian Metaphysical Minister in 1990, I realized an ancient personal dream. Within a year, I became an inspired speaker, guided directly by spirit, just as my father had done centuries before. Gabriel made it clear that there are no coincidences, no accidents. We plan our lives and everyone and every situation we encounter. His visitations began the same year I started studying for the ministry. My head was clearing then, with three years of sobriety behind me. Gabriel said that because our soul contains the memory of every experience of every past lifetime, when we encounter a painful situation again our soul recalls what happened the last time - whether last year or last incarnation - and we are filled with trepidation, or turn away from it. It is not in our conscious memory; we aren't aware of the reason for our trepidation. About the time I was ordained I began to have trouble with my left hip, and the increasing pain resulted in an obvious limp in my walk. I tolerated this situation for six years, seeking various alternate healing methods to cure it. None did. A chiropractor, an acupuncturist and a gemstone healer all alleviated the discomfort temporarily but finally I succumbed to the idea of surgery for a total hip replacement. My recovery was speedy and I have never had any more pain with it. Prior to the surgery, I risked telling my primary physician and the surgeon the metaphysical basis for the hip problem. They both listened intently without comment, which pleased me greatly. Perhaps I had planted a seed of truth. Gabriel had made it clear that behind every physical ailment there is a metaphysical cause. God created us to be healthy, joyous and have abundance. Only our thinking, our error-perceptions, cause illness, disease, poverty and unhappiness.

In the case of my total hip replacement in 1998, the metaphysical explanation is, as a female child, I was not valued, as explained in the first chapter. The left side of the body is the female (nurturing) side; the right side of the physical form is the male (action) side. The legs represent moving forward. My soul's memory recalled the early death for heresy centuries before (500 AD) and I became fearful of serving God again. The idea of becoming a minister manifested as a painful reminder of the past. At some level of my consciousness, I believed that I was not worthy to serve God.

As I contemplated Gabriel's teachings about planning our lives, I wondered why I had chosen to be homosexual. Let me say here that although in my later years I preferred making love to women, I was sexually satisfied in those 22 years I lived with my husband. One might say that I am bisexual. By our very nature, psychologists tell us that we all are.

Gabriel, through all the years of his teaching, welcomed questions. Thus, it was that I asked Gabriel why some people are gay. He provided us with two possible explanations:

Firstly, after each incarnation on earth (reincarnation is *always* species specific), we review our life and judge ourselves as to what we learned and what we failed to learn in the just-completed lifetime, based on our plan prior to birth. When we spend a lifetime - or several lifetimes - with an attitude of fear and hatred toward homosexuals, we decide consciously while on the other side, before our next birth, to live as a homosexual in order to learn the lessons of tolerance and understanding.

Secondly, in the case where we have spent many lifetimes as one sex and then desire to live a lifetime as the opposite sex, it is essential that we take the time to harmonize our energy field with the energy field of that sex. Failing to take sufficient time to do this, results in birthing in a body of one sex but having the desires of the other sex.

One time Gabriel said to us, you have only one life. There was a sudden gasp from the audience. Quickly he added that the one life is the life of our spirit, our eternal Self. We choose many experiences, called earthly lifetimes, to learn. Recalling that lesson, I sought to comprehend the meaning for my affliction with alcoholism. One possible explanation is that as an alcoholic in a previous life, I chose to return to continue the indulgence. Perhaps I agreed to return with others of that mind, which would explain the fact that at least three of my siblings (four of nine kids) were also alcoholics. In the course of my alcoholism, I was viciously judgmental. This brings me to a past life not mentioned previously. It is the one most difficult to admit. Gabriel himself told it to me one evening as he offered a question and answer session. He mentioned that we all are working on an issue from a past life (karma). Someone went to the microphone and asked Gabriel to tell her what issue of a past life she was working on. Knowing human nature as he does, he said, "If I tell you, beloved woman, I would have to tell everyone". The rest of the group in unison said, "Yes, tell us, too!" Gabriel acquiesced, and told the person at the recording machine to turn it off. It was the one and only time he took this action, in the 12 years of his visitations. He knew that what he was about to impart was personal and should be kept private. He went around the room to each person, describing a past incarnation and telling us what lesson we had chosen to learn this time around.

I was not ready for what he said to me, but I knew and still know that only truth came from him. He said that I was Mary I, Queen of England. As the Catholic Mary Tudor, I was known as Bloody Mary because I executed over a hundred Protestants, including six churchmen whom I had burned at the stake. Gabriel told me another name I was called was Queen of the Guillotine. I shuddered at this tragic knowledge of what I had been, especially when he said Bloody Mary, for it was the name of one of my favorite drinks during my years of alcoholism. The lesson (one of them) in this lifetime is for me to learn to overcome the ferocious judgmentalism of Queen Mary and those alcoholic years.

At some point in the course of Gabriel's twelve years of teaching us, we asked him about the habit of eating meat. What he told us sent a shiver down my spine. He said that eons ago, when man first inhabited the earth, we were eating only nature's harvest. We were vegetarians. Then, from outer space, came a group of entities who told us that it was good to eat meat. Because they came from the sky, we thought they were gods and followed their advice. We began eating, and continue to eat, flesh. Gabriel explained their real motive. The aliens came not to teach us, but rather to find flesh, the food they were used to eating. They had run out of meat on their own planet to the point where they had started eating each other. They decided to investigate the planet earth, and found a great variety of animals here. Gabriel *never* instructed us not to eat meat. He did tell us that as creatures are slaughtered they scream and others of their kind in the abattoir hear the screams. The screams reflect their fear, and the fear vibration permeates their flesh.

Gabriel recommended that we eat fresh fruit and vegetables as well as grains and nuts. Spending several minutes on nutrition one day, he said that produce grown in our home area is best because of its vibrational harmony with our bodies. In the preparation of food, he suggested raw was best, then steamed, then frozen. And canned food was the least desirable. Prepared foods contain too many chemicals to be healthy. Soon I stopped eating red meat, but I occasionally eat a dish with some meat in it, like chili con carne. At this point, I continue to eat fish and fowl.

As an avid student of Gabriel, I shared with many others an eager enthusiasm to learn the wisdom of the ages that he imparted to us. At one time, he said that he had told us all this information before - 500 years before! We must have been together as a group in the fifteenth century somewhere. He did not say where. To be perfectly honest, there was a time about two years after he began teaching us that I had some doubts about his veracity. Could this be some kind of *cult?* Then I decided that I would give him more time to determine if he was consistent in his message, caring in his approach and willing to continue answering all our questions. Did his teachings make sense and could I put them to use in my daily life? His message was the opposite of what a cult is: a set of exclusive beliefs by a sequestered group, who are encouraged to worship their leader and are forbidden to mingle with outsiders. Gabriel, on the other hand, gave us profound messages that withstood analysis.

Moreover, he told us to think about the lessons, apply them to our lives and prove to ourselves their validity. He recommended that we question everything he said, to understand fully his words and reasoning. Truth needs no defense, he said. Learn the truth and share it with others willing to hear. He made it clear to us that he did not want a following; he did not come to start something new, he did not seek a following for Rev. Penny. He came to tell us who and what we really are: children of God, asleep to our own sacred core. He was a messenger from God who came to wake us up to our own divinity so that we could live from that center, made in the image of God as told in Scripture.

Many lessons of Gabriel were about the stories in Scripture. His topics included the true meaning of Christmas, the Easter story, the crucifixion and its true meaning, the story of the prodigal son as the story of Jesus himself. He gave us details of the story of Judith, described Jesus Christ and spoke at length about his life, his intent and his resurrection. He said the book of Revelation is not about the end of the world but rather every person's singular path back home to God. As with the rest of Scripture, Revelation is full of symbolism, a primary teaching tool of the Bible. He confirmed that *A Course in Miracles* was written by Jesus through a faithful channel and written down by a faithful scribe. As noted in that book, Gabriel also reminded us that in the story of Eden, Adam fell asleep - yet nowhere in Scripture does it say that Adam woke up! Yes, we are still asleep to our own origin of spirit. Our every cell has a spiritual nucleus. We are in fact light beings, created by the Father of lights. (James I: 17)

One of the questions I put to Gabriel was Paul's phrase, "thorn in the flesh," found in II Corinthians 7-8): *And lest I should be exalted above measure through the abundance of the revelations, there was given to me a thorn in the flesh . . . lest I should be exalted above measure. For this thing, I besought the Lord thrice, that it might depart from me.*

When I asked Gabriel what the thorn was, he said Paul was what you call today a gay person, " . . . though I don't know why; they rarely seem happy."

When I decided to write my second book, it was my original intent to write only about Gabriel's teachings, but when I sent five chapters to my editor she said it was not what she expected, did not have enough Ellen in it and it would not sell. Only slightly discouraged I prayed for guidance. The message soon came to me, Write to your grandchildren and your children. It was clear that I could tell the story of my spiritual path best by telling about my life leading up to it.

At one time Archangel Gabriel confirmed that Jesus Christ had indeed given Helen Shucman the information which appears in *A Course in Miracles* (1975). It is a required course for all of humanity. The curriculum is the same for everyone, only the time to learn it is our choice. Jesus began channeling through Rev. Penny in 1995. At Christmas of that year he presented a talk on "The True Meaning of Christmas." It was December 3, 1995 and he closed with the following prayer:

My Father, I thank Thee that Thou has given unto me these my brethren, these fellow children. I thank Thee that they have allowed me to enter into their consciousness to come into the world of their creation. I give You thanks that I might take their hand and lead them, that I might touch them and heal them, that I might laugh with them, and love with them, and cause them to be as I Am, in You forever. I bid you a good evening of your time.

For information and to order audiocassettes and
written lessons of Archangel Gabriel: email:
appleseeds@hvc.rr.com and virgilmc@hvc.rr.com
and www.apathtoGod.com

FAMILY TREE

Ida Mae Armstrong	Robert Bruce Wallace
1890-1965	1875-1934

Marcia Ruth	1910
Ada Beth	1912
Robert Bruce	1913
Charles Blake	1915
Leah Jane	1918
Phyllis Joy	1921
Mertice Evelyn	1923
Alvin Armstrong	1924

Ellen Rae and	Stephen Albert Douglas
1928 -	1912 - 1989

Evaline Ann	1950

Owen Raymond
Stephanie Rae-Ellen

Roy Stewart no children	1952
Martin Wallace	1954

Nicholas Watkins
Shane Christian
Jillian Joy

Wendy Jean	1957

Jeffrey Stephen
Bryan James
Michael David
Katie Joy